Catalina Island

All You Need To Know

Joe Belanger

AUTHOR: **Joe Belanger**

FRONT COVER: **Cameron Black** (cameron@californiaunderwater.com)
Cheryl Vowell (cheryl@californiaunderwater.com)

DESIGNER: **H. Donald Kroitzsh**

Published by:
Roundtable Publishing
P O Box 13424
Mesa, AZ 85216
co-op email: sales@californiaunderwater.com
co-op website: www.californiaunderwater.com
Telephone: 480-354-1063/714-620-6085

Printed in the United States of America

Designed by:
Five Corners Publications, Ltd.
5052 Route 100
Plymouth, Vermont 05056   USA
books@fivecorners.com

CATALINA ISLAND — ALL YOU NEED TO KNOW
Library of Congress Card Number: 00-190798
ISBN: 0-970008-60-0

In memory of **Laura Stein**,
who gave her entire heart and soul
to the conservation and management of Catalina's interior.

FOREWORD

Joe Belanger has complied an excellent resource book which he has appropriately titled *Catalina Island, All You Need to Know*. This is not just a fine diving guide, it is also a "how-to-do-it" kit for getting there, where to stay and what to do, along with interesting sections on both human and natural history. Catalina is the most often dove island near the continental United States, as it has the optimum combination of clear calm water and businesses to support diving. Of course, this is still a well done dive guide, with the most accurate and detailed dive site data available, plus an informative chapter on marine life and another well researched section on the dive history at Catalina. Joe has done his homework in putting together this wealth of information, along with outstanding color photography. The book is assembled in an easy to access and use format – much of the dive information is not available anywhere else. *Catalina Island, All You Need to Know*, can be used as both a vacation/holiday planning guide and as a traveling guide to tuck away in your backpack. Another extremely useful aspect of this book is that it gives a full detailed range of activities for your non-diving friends and family. Catalina is a place to be experienced both above and below the water, and this handy volume helps you do just that.

Jon Hardy, Director of ScubaLab
Santa Catalina Island
May 2000

REFERENCES

Behrens, D. (1980), *Pacific Coast Nudibranchs,*
    Los Osos, CA: Sea Challengers

Daily, M. (1987), *California's Channel Islands,*
    Santa Barbara, CA: Kimberly Press, Inc.

Eschmeyer, W., Herald, E., & Hammann, H. (1983),
    A Field Guide to Pacific Coast Fishes,
    Boston, MA: Houghton Mifflin Company

Gilliam, B. (1995), *Deep Diving,*
    San Diego, CA: Watersport Publishing

Gotchall, D., & Laurent, L. (1979),
    Pacific Coast Subtidal Marine Invertebrates,
    Los Osos, CA: Sea Challengers

Knopf, A. (1981), *The Audubon Society Field Guide to North America,*
    New York, NY: Chanticleer Press, Inc.

Martin, T. (1983), *Santa Catalina, An Island Adventure,*
    Las Vegas, NV: KC Publications, Inc.

Moore, P. (1979), *Casino,*
    Avalon, CA: Catalina Island Museum Society.

Morris, R., Abbott, D., & Haderlie, E. (1980),
    Intertidal Invertebrates of California,
    Stanford, CA: Stanford University Press

ACKNOWLEDGMENTS

My sincere gratitude goes to a variety of unique individuals who over several years unselfishly contributed their time and effort to this book. Jon Hardy of Argo Diving Services provided a foundation from which the dive site section was written. Jon shared with me decades of diving knowledge and provided important insight that would have not been otherwise available for my use. Bob & Tina Kennedy of Catalina Diving Resorts also provided key information as it related to Catalina's underwater world, as did John Mello of Catalina Divers Supply. My sincere gratitude goes out to all of them.

Thanks to Catalina Conservancy member Laura Stein, who graciously shared with me her vast knowledge of Catalina's floral community and helped me understand why conservation was necessary. I am also indebted to Randy Bombard, former manager of the Two Harbors operation, for the resources he provided during this project. Many thanks to island naturalist Steve Whittington, who guided me through much of Catalina's terrain during several photo safaris.

Thanks to these individuals on Catalina and the mainland who graciously shared their services and knowledge: Martin Curtin, Joe Caliva, Mary Stein, Randy Brannock, Glynis Herbel, Mike Farrior, Misty Gay, Patricia Moore, Rudy Pilch, Cindy Spring, Rosellen Gardner and Chuck Oleson. A special thanks goes to the following diving pioneers who contributed a wealth of stories and facts about Catalina: Mart Toggweiler, Zale Parry, Ron Merker, Chuck Blakeslee, Harold Warner, John Gaffney, and Andy Pilmanis.

Years after I became scuba certified, I hooked up with professional diver and marine biologist Mike Curtis. Mike showed me a lot about diving responsibility, techniques, and marine life. We also used his boat, Deep Freak, to dive Catalina numerable times. I can't count the good memories I have of those trips. Gracias, Mike. My diving career and sense of adventure has also been positively influenced by professional diver and author Eric Hanauer, who has provided a potpourri of meaningful and helpful opinions ranging from photography to writing to travel. I have spent countless hours diving Catalina with Eric. We always have our cameras with us and frequently compare results, discuss photographic techniques, and talk shop. As a result, I have become a better photographer and diver. Shukran, Eric.

Thanks to my parents, Vic and Opal, who made this book possible by standing behind my diving antics after I became involved in the hobby when I was sixteen. Finally, I'd like to acknowledge my best friend, Bob McDonald, who is responsible for introducing me to Catalina and the sport of scuba diving in 1976.

PREFACE

My love for Catalina was born during my first diving sojourn there in 1976. After making numerable dive trips to the island, I developed an inescapable passion for its underwater world. To me, Catalina was scuba diving, laying out on my buddy's sailboat, and listening to good music. Night times were special, too. I'd stretch out on the sailboat bow, bundle up in a sleeping bag, and listen to the sounds of pinging lanyards echoing across the bay—usually underneath a sky full of stars. To me, nothing was more relaxing.

This acquired island lifestyle didn't change for several years until I decided to spend a weekend on Catalina, without the sailboat and scuba gear. Considering my memorable aquatic adventures thus far, I was happy with the Catalina I knew. But after setting foot on the island, I discovered a new source for adventure and contentment. Today, some of my best island memories come from visiting Catalina's interior, cruising Avalon's hills in a golf cart, and eating scrumptious strawberry French toast at the Pancake Cottage.

Catalina's enticing underwater scenery is without question paralleled by its terrestrial lore and excitement. With so much history and quality entertainment, Catalina is an excellent option for those looking for an exciting getaway.

Catalina Island, All You Need to Know, details tourist information about Catalina's diving world and its terrestrial wonders. The book's first section is an all encompassing tour guide, detailing information about transportation, lodging, dining, island activities, and tours. Each of these chapters includes a handy quick reference intended to eliminate the hassle of having to sift through pages of text to find specific phone numbers and related reference material.

Additionally, to provide insight into island history and lore, I have inserted several chapters that discuss points of interest and island history. Chapter one looks at Catalina from its formation to its modern day reality. Chapter two reviews climate and basic physiography. And chapter six chronicles significant points of interest, such as how the glass bottom boat evolved and the building of Holly Hill House.

The diving section of the guidebook is a first. With the help of many diving professionals, I have put together a complete dive guide that includes information on 56 Catalina dive sites, including their latitude and longitude coordinates. This section is partly intended to offer information allowing those with private boats to find the same diving sites that charter boats visit. Also, island diving operations and mainland dive charter services that visit Catalina are reviewed. The last chapter focuses on marine life and discusses the animals that divers routinely see while underwater.

Keeping a guide book of this capacity up to date is not easy, especially when considering how fast Catalina is growing. Even during the production of this book, new island restaurants emerged and several innovative tours were introduced. Although our intention is to update this guide periodically, a supplemental Visitor's Guide is available from Catalina's Chamber of Commerce. The Visitor's Guide is updated annually to include changes as they relate to island businesses.

When using this extensive guidebook, travelers can plan a complete day, weekend, or week long stay at Catalina without collecting dozens of brochures. It is a tool specifically designed to eliminate frustration and add pleasure and excitement to your island vacation.

CONTENTS

HISTORY & DEVELOPMENT

Additional Internet Information
http://www.catalina.com/history.html

Catalina Island has a colorful history, beginning with its birth millions of years ago right up to modern day. Many visitors, however, come to the island with almost no knowledge of its geology, biology and historical events. This chapter briefly chronicles Catalina's evolution.

Catalina's development has created a playground of excitement and visitor accommodation. This is Avalon in the late 1800's. (Photo Courtesy of SCICo)

An Island Is Born

Santa Catalina Island evolved nearly 100 million years ago when long periods of geologic and volcanic activity uplifted material from the sea floor, ultimately forming a virgin island just 20 miles from the shore of Los Angeles. The island's unique geometric shape, coupled with the ocean's climatic influences, laid the groundwork for evolution to create a truly unique ecosystem.

A series of craggy rock patterns and hillsides formed on the surface of this newly born island. Over time, several natural processes brought small animals and seeds of varying types to Catalina. Eventually, within the confines of these peaks, valleys and shear drop-offs, an array of unique plant and animal communities emerged, forming a geographically restricted ecosystem.

Similar evolutionary processes brought a kingdom of rich life to the island's underwater world. The formation of enormous passageways, walls, caves, outcrops and bottom compositions provided unusual habitats from which truly interesting aquatic animals evolved. Thus time presented a beautiful display of both terrestrial and marine plants and animals, all framed by twisted rock formations, green pastures and metallic-blue water. Loaded with promise, it was simply a factor of time before humans would embrace Catalina as their home.

Catalina Indians

Over a span of 7,000 years, various native American groups inhabited Catalina. The most recent were the Gabrieliño, the subject of this segment. The Gabrieliño enjoyed a secluded lifestyle, living primarily off the riches of the island and its surrounding waters. They called themselves "Pimugnans" and their island "Pimu" or "Pimugna." Being efficient dwellers, the Indians lived in large, 50 to 60 foot diameter huts that held several families. Their lifestyle consisted primarily of fishing and trading, which in part explains their shoreline residency. The island's abundant marine resources were a bounteous source of food for the natives; inshore invertebrates, mammals and fish were regularly consumed.

Though Pimugna lacked many resources necessary for survival, the native population capitalized on abundant amounts of soapstone (steatite) found in local quarries. Soapstone is a soft, metamorphic rock that, when heated, seldom cracks—ideal for cooking. Because mainland soapstone quarries were scarce, Pimugnans possessed a valuable commodity sought by their cross channel counterparts.

Pimugnans lived a peaceful, secluded lifestyle along the shores of Catalina. They lived in huts that accommodated two or three families.

Islanders crafted many items of importance to the coastal Indians including **ollas**, or stone cooking bowls, and similar utensils. A lucrative trade market was subsequently organized, by which Pimugnans swapped soapstone goods for hides, food and other necessary supplies.

Pimugnans were involved in a flourishing trade market with mainland tribes, swapping ollas (similar to this one) for other items such as furs.

The Pimugnans encountered their first foreign visitors, the Spanish expedition of Juan Rodriguez Cabrillo, when the explorers arrived on Pimu the morning of October 7, 1542. The Indians extended a warm welcome offering the newcomers food and a place to rest. Though Cabrillo's island visit lasted only half a day, he chronicled his discovery in a daily log, one entry of which included a name for the newfound island: San Salvador (the name of his flagship).

Cabrillo died shortly after his departure. The diary that documented his daily trials and tribulations (including the naming of San Salvador) found its way into the doldrums of Spain, where it lay forgotten until more recent times. Experts believe this is why the name Cabrillo bestowed to the island never endured.

It was not until sixty years later, in 1602, that Spanish explorer Sebastiàn Vizcaíno would rediscover Pimugna and pronounce a new and lasting name. Since Vizcaíno's visit occurred during the feast day of Saint Catherine of Alexandria (November 25, 1602), he christened the island St. Caterina (Catalina) in her honor. It is ironic that this island of romance received its name in honor of the patron saint of maidens, St. Catherine.

The Pimugnans prosperity ended in the 1800s, when an influx of misery chiseled away at their entire existence. They suffered their first significant tragedy when a measles epidemic broke out and took the lives of nearly 200 islanders. Historians believe that further population decline came when the Pimugnans' trade economy was disrupted by the mainland mission system. Because the padres became active in merchandising pottery and other competitive goods, the Indians gradually drifted to the mainland. Some joined missions while others established a village near the Pueblo of Los Angeles. As time passed, many Pimugnans inter-married and melded into the general public. The white man's way of life, however, proved to be detrimental to the relocated Indians; many died after contracting syphilis, small pox and other dreaded diseases.

A Smugglers Base

During the Spanish occupation of California in the early 1800s, Catalina served predominantly as a base for smugglers, particularly after the War of 1812; contraband activities skyrocketed because the Spanish government closed every California port to all foreign vessels. Yankee traders unwilling to bear the sanctions began a profusion of illegal trading activities along the Pacific coast. Unlawful bartering activity was so intense that the Spaniards were unable to regulate it.

After 1820, Spanish rule gave way to Mexican occupation of California, but illegal trading still persisted. Since tariffs were the Mexican Government's only source of revenue, they established a customshouse at Monterey, California in 1821. Ships with cargo would stop at this post, pay cargo duty, then be on their way to trade freely along the coast. The Mexicans set tariffs at 100 percent of the value of the declared merchandise; this provoked many trade-merchant to look for ways to circumvent the system. Skippers, fed-up and frustrated, began to smuggle most of their valuable goods past customs to avoid paying high duty. This is when Catalina Island became a smuggling Eden; a cove was even named after the activity: Smugglers Cove.

Skippers avoided paying duty using several tricks. A common method was to unload the expensive merchandise at various coves around Catalina. The captain would leave a group of sailors to guard the cache, sail on to Monterey where he would declare his diminished supply of goods, pay the tariff, then sail back to the island to retrieve his goods. Though the trip to Monterey lasted several days, it was worth the smuggler's trouble; now having documentation that he paid his rightful share, trading along the coast commenced without worry of being nabbed by authorities.

Another way to beat the system was trading among smugglers. When a ship captain began to run low on his duty-paid goods, he would set up a rendezvous in one of Catalina's small cove's with a newly arriving trader. The captain would purchase the goods from the new arrival, and then continue his bartering affairs along the coast using his old duty voucher. In the end, both parties profited by dodging the expenditures of lofty tariffs. When California became part of the U.S. in 1848, the trading situation changed and free trade was finally granted. However, five years later, in 1853, smugglers used Catalina Island as a trafficking refuge for Chinese laborers. The contrabandists held quietly until such a time they could safely smuggle the foreigners to the mainland and put them to work.

The Development of Avalon

Paralleling the smuggling efforts of the latter 1800s, island ownership changed hands several times. In 1846, two years before the Mexican War, the Mexican Government deeded Catalina to Thomas Robbins of Santa Barbara, a naturalized Mexican citizen. After Robbins, the next recorded owner was Don Nicolas Covarrubias who purchased the island for $10,000. After that, a lawyer from Santa Barbara named Albert Packard received the island dirt cheap, paying only $1,000 for it. Though Packard resold portions of Catalina to various individuals, James Lick, founder of the Lick Observatory, pieced together the various sales and finally acquired the entire island as a single deed in 1867. He paid a total of $92,000.

Entrepreneur George Shatto (Photo courtesy of SCICo).

One of Catalina's most notable transactions took place in 1887 when investors of the Lick estate resold Catalina for $200,000 to George Shatto. Shatto, a businessman and entrepreneur, was perhaps ultimately responsible for the Catalina we know today. He intended to turn the island into a tourist resort, beginning his five year reign by surveying the land and building a hotel. To expand Avalon's tourist base further, Shatto used steamships he leased from the Bannings to ferry tourists to and from the mainland. Some island tourists arrived to purchase lots in Avalon, which Shatto auctioned off for $150 to $2,000 depending on location and size. Those who purchased one were then free to set up tents or build summer cottages.

When George Shatto purchased Catalina in 1887, he first built the Hotel Metropole, which was used mostly to accommodate potential real estate customers (Photo courtesy of SCICo).

However, in the midst of Shatto's promotional scheme, he racked up some hefty bills and defaulted on his mortgage payments. The Lick Trust, to which Shatto made his payments, took the island back. The Lick trust resold Catalina in 1892 for $128,740 to the Banning brothers, sons of stagecoach monarch, General Phineas Banning.

Avalon essentially became a tent city after investors who purchased property lots set up tent cottages (Photo courtesy of SCICo).

Though the onset of Avalon's development was Shatto's doing, the Bannings, together with other entrepreneurs, made more significant accomplishments shortly after their acquisition. The Banning family first formed an island management corporation called the Santa Catalina Island Company. The purpose of the corporation was to manage the transformation of Catalina into a tourist retreat. Hoping that they would fulfill the early dreams of Shatto, the Bannings began developing the City of Avalon.

Over a span of 23 years, the Bannings built commuter roads throughout the island's interior, ran glass-bottom boat tours regularly, and vigorously promoted sport fishing with the help of fishing buff, Charles Frederick Holder. In 1913, Avalon was incorporated as Los Angeles County's 30th city. However, after a series of hardships, including

The streets of Avalon in 1895 (Photo courtesy of SCICo).

a fire in 1915 that destroyed about a third of the city, the Bannings decided to sell.

The Avalon fire of 1915 destroyed about one third of the city. This photo shows the burned down Motel Metropole (Photo courtesy of SCICo).

In 1919, chewing gum giant William Wrigley, of Chicago, Illinois gained ownership of Catalina after purchasing controlling interest in the Santa Catalina Island Company. His genuine respect for natural beauty and historical relevance led him to treat and manage the island as a natural wilderness, thus discouraging development farther than the boundaries of Avalon.

It was Wrigley's intention to fulfill the dreams of his predecessors and redevelop Avalon. He began to sink millions of dollars into island improvements; an example is a $2,500,000 tab just to solve the water quandary. He built an exquisite bird park, from which visitors could observe many colorful and exotic species. Wrigley, then owner of the Chicago

William Wrigley Jr.
(Photo courtesy of SCICo).

Cubs, even built a baseball field on the island so he could bring his team over each year for spring training.

These types of innovative improvements, over the next 13 years until his death, helped Wrigley accomplish his goal: to build a world-class island resort that beckoned visitors from all walks of life.

His most prized accomplishment was the construction of the famed Casino in 1929, which Wrigley figured would improve his revenues by attracting more tourists. Though the Casino was never used for gambling, it was a place for people to gather and enjoy some camaraderie and entertainment. It held a variety of functions following its grand opening, but the Casino's earmark during this era was ballroom dancing to the live music of big bands.

With the fruition of the Casino emerged a blossoming tourist base. Many flocked the island to see this monumental attraction, which was William Wrigley's original intention. However, this tourist growth demanded more from other island businesses, specifically the glass bottom boat trade. By

The Chicago Cubs at Catalina in the 1920's (Photo courtesy of SCICo).

1931, the Santa Catalina Island Company added five glass bottom boats to their fleet to handle increased tourism. It was readily apparent that the charms of Catalina's fruitful underwater world cast a shadow of value on the tourist market.

The Benny Goodman band is but one of many big bands that played at Catalina's Casino Ballroom (Photo courtesy of SCICo).

By 1943, this circle of adventure would heighten with the invention of the Aqualung regulator. The idea of a self-contained underwater breathing apparatus (scuba) free of surface support, where one could venture underwater at free will, was a milestone commodity that would serve to augment Catalina's tourist market in later years. The life-rich waters surrounding Catalina over time attracted a

In addition to bringing glass bottom boats to Catalina, Wrigley also brought the Blanch W to the island. This vessel was used for tours such as flying fish journeys (Photo courtesy of SCICo).

new type of sportsman: the scuba diver. Over a span of 50 years, Catalina has become a high profile California diving destination, escalating its annual tourist base by thousands.

Catalina Today

Today, Avalon remains Catalina's principal tourist attraction. Though nearly 20 miles separate this unique town from the mainland, remoteness has not altered progress. Catalina contains all essential utilities such as electricity, water and phones. Rainwater is stored in reservoirs throughout the island's interior, which is purified and piped to the towns of Avalon and Two Harbors. A desalination plant also supplies water to Avalon during periods of drought. All electricity and water services are furnished by the Edison Company, while Pacific Bell provides telephone utilities.

Historic Eagles Nest lodge stands as a memento of Catalina's past.

Avalon is, nevertheless, only a small part of Catalina's history and enchantment; its 75 square miles of interior wilderness is a symbol of what California was like long ago, offering fantastic blends of plant and animal life-forms that are now uncommon on the mainland. Additional interests include roaming bison which were introduced to Catalina in the early 1900's. The island's historic sites, such as Eagles Nest Lodge, also continue to serve as mementos of Catalina's bygone era.

Though Catalina today is only slightly exploited for some of its resources, conservationists see to it that the natural state of the island and its historical sites remain protected and properly managed, as Wrigley had originally envisioned. This conservation effort was realized in 1974 when the Santa Catalina Island Company signed a 50 year

Like Catalina Conservancy, Catalina Conservancy Divers helps maintain the quality of marine life at Catalina.

Catalina' has developed into a playground of excitement, beauty, and visitor accommodation.

easement with the county of Los Angeles, handing over most of the island acreage for recreation and conservation.

About a year later, the Santa Catalina Island Conservancy, a nonprofit organization committed to maintaining, restoring and managing natural and historic sites, acquired most of the holdings as a gift from the Wrigley family, and now owns approximately 86 percent (roughly 42,000 acres) of Catalina. It is the Conservancy's ongoing goal to preserve native plants and animals, biotic communities, open space lands and geological and geographical entities important to the educational and recreational interests of the public.

One of the many support groups, the Catalina Conservancy Divers, cares for much of the island's surrounding waters, focusing on protecting, restoring and conserving Catalina's marine environment. Projects such as reestablishing abalone populations and sponsoring underwater cleanups are but a few of their responsibilities.

The Catalina Conservancy and Conservancy Divers are independent organizations. They rely heavily on private donations and fund raising activities as primary sources of revenue. Ultimately, though, it is the love and respect Conservancy personnel have for the island that has helped Catalina to remain a true time capsule where visitors can tour through years of island history, and divers can enjoy the excitement of its underwater world.

PRACTICAL INFORMATION

Additional Internet Information
http://www.catalina.com/chamber.html

Catalina's Physiography & Geology

Two basic rock types make up the geologic structure of Catalina Island. The first element is composed of igneous (volcanic) rock and is most prevalent toward the east end of the island. Western Catalina consists primarily of metamorphic (compressed) rock. These rock types combine to make the third largest of California's eight Channel Islands. Catalina is 21 miles (33.8 km) long and poised in a northwest to southeast direction. Its

The narrow stretch between Catalina Harbor and Isthmus Cove is less than a half mile.

widest stretch is eight miles (12.9 km), measured from Long Point to China Point, while its narrowest section at Two Harbors (Isthmus) is just under one-half mile (.85 km).

When Cabrillo first visited Catalina (then called Pimugna by the Catalina Indians) he actually thought it was two separate islands because of the pronounced drop in elevation at Two Harbors. Only until Cabrillo moved his ship in proximity to the cove did he realize Catalina was indeed one island.

Today, geodetic surveys tell the story of Catalina's size. It covers an expanse of approximately 75 square miles (120.5 km), and encompasses 54 miles (86.8 km) of coastline. Its highest point is Mt. Orizaba (2,069 feet or 630 m), followed by Mt. Black Jack which rises to just over 2,000 feet (610 m). Catalina is personified largely by steep mountains and rugged valleys, while a considerable portion of its geology comprises open meadows and rolling hills.

Along Catalina's shoreline, the geology is characterized by steep-faced drop-offs that fall directly into the blue water below, leaving virtually no beaches at waters edge. Small, isolated coves with coarse sand and cobblestone beaches characterize other areas, while some shoreline regions are earmarked by prehistoric, wave-cut terraces and jumbled boulders.

At Catalina's airport is a large tile map of the island, highlighting many island features, such as mountains, property lines and notable locations.

In all, the basic geology of Catalina is inconsistent, diverse, and constantly changing. Scientists report that changes in sea level, together with periodic uplift and downdrop, has altered the island's size at various times. A submerged terrace, extending about one mile seaward, is evidence that Catalina was once a much larger island. Even today, changes occur via landslides, geologic uplift and shoreline erosion.

Calm weather shows the serenity of Avalon harbor.

Climate

Summertime offers the most consistent climate at Catalina. The days are usually warm and sunny, and evenings cool, yet comfortable. Interruptive weather fronts are seldom a problem during summer, which is partly accountable for the large crowds typical of this season. Winter, on the other hand, offers the most climatic variety. In fact, while Catalina receives the bulk of its 14 inch (5.5 cm) annual downpour during this season, experiencing winter sunshine for days or weeks at a time is common.

Because of the surrounding ocean, fog and overcast skies are year-round occurrences. Marine layers of fog might show up in early morning and evening; it may also linger the entire day, especially during winter and early spring. Additionally, recurrent sea breezes help to cool sultry days or make chilly ones seem colder than they really are. As a whole, though, influence of the marine environment is the catalyst for keeping Catalina a few degrees cooler than the mainland during summertime, and a bit warmer when winter arrives.

Fog is commonly encountered at Catalina. Here, during an early morning interior tour, fog shadows some of Catalina's bison.

A climatic surprise repeatedly encountered at Catalina is how quickly temperatures fall when the sun sets. Temperatures may be 75° (23.8° C) in Avalon during the daytime, but after the sun tucks itself behind the towering hillsides, front side temperatures often drop by nearly 10° (3.7C°) within an hour. This condition is bedeviled further when late afternoon sea breezes and fog

During the peak summer season, Catalina's population increases dramatically. One of the more popular activities during this exciting time of year is sun bathing.

befall the island. As a general rule, visitors should dress according to the weather. Just keep in mind that nighttimes at Catalina can become unexpectedly cool.

Catalina Facts

Topic	Fact	Notes
Distance from Mainland	21.8 miles (35 km)	Measured from San Pedro Breakwater to Avalon.
Length of Island	21 miles (33.7 km)	N/A
Widest Point	8 miles (12.9 km)	Measured from China Point to Long Point
Narrowest Point	1/2 mile (.8 km)	Measured from Cat Harbor to Isthmus Cove
Highest Point	2,069 feet (630.6 m)	Measured from Mt. Orizaba
Island Perimeter	54 miles (86.9 km)	Approximate
Total Acreage	47,884 (193,786,548 sq. m)	Coverage is approximate
Total Square Miles	76 (197 sq. km)	Coverage is approximate
Distance: Avalon to Two Harbors	13.4 miles (21.5 km)	By boat
Distance: Avalon to Two Harbors	23 miles (37 km)	By inland road

Average Temperatures:

	(°F) H / L	(°C) H / L	
January	63 / 49	17 / 9	Average figures
February	62 / 49	17 / 9	
March	61 / 50	16 / 10	
April	65 / 53	18 / 12	
May	67 / 54	20 / 12	
June	70 / 57	21 / 14	
July	73 / 61	23 / 16	
August	72 / 62	22 / 17	
September	74 / 61	23 / 16	
October	73 / 58	23 / 15	
November	70 / 53	21 / 12	
December	63 / 46	17 / 8	

Average Seasonal Temperatures

Season	Months	Average Daytime Temperature °F/°C	Average Nighttime Temperature °F/°C
Summer	June 21-September 23	72 / 22	60 / 15.5
Fall	September 24-December 20	72 / 22	57 / 14
Winter	December 21-March 19	62 / 16.5	49 / 9
Spring	March 20-June 20	66 / 19	54 / 12

About the Seasons

Summer: Catalina's peak visitor base occurs during summer break, from June to September, when southland families frequent the island. Consequently there's a dramatic increase in island population from its off-season average of 3,000 to more than 10,000 on weekends. Tourists should prepare themselves to cope with lines and crowds.

Fall: After school starts, Catalina crowds diminish. You can typically find the best weather during the fall, without the lines. And island businesses, some of which close during the winter, are still open to serve visitors.

Winter: During periods of winter sunshine, there's a significant advantage to visiting Catalina. It is an ideal time to miss the crowds, maintain a certain level of seclusion, and obtain frugally priced tour and hotel packages. However, wintertime is an economic thorn-in-the-foot for many island businesses. Because the crowds are meager, incoming revenue typically declines, forcing some establishments to operate only on the weekends and others to close until spring arrives.

Spring: In spite of recurrent overcast conditions during springtime, Catalina's herbage is overwhelming. Sun position and temperature during this season, coupled with winter rains, create an island greenhouse of deep colors and wild shapes. Spring brings out the best of Catalina's horticultural showcase by hosting a magnificent display of wildflowers and incredibly green pastures and rolling hills. It is also the season to see newly born bison as they trot happily by their mothers' sides.

The benefit of modest crowds, mild temperatures, and colorful island scenery are sound reasons for visiting Catalina during this season. Moreover, most businesses have opened their doors to prepare for summer demand and consequently offer terrific off season packages.

Air Quality

Typically, Catalina experiences very little smog. Common westerly winds keep most of the unhealthy air pushed up against the mainland and because the island is 20 miles from the coastline, smog rarely affects it. Exceptions occur, however, during Santa Ana wind conditions. As wind is forced out to sea from distant inland deserts and mountains, so is coastal smog. However, because the foul air is spread out over the large ocean, Catalina doesn't sustain the concentrations typical of the mainland.

Vast fields of wildflowers line the hills of Catalina during springtime. It is an unsurpassed sensation to hear gently blowing breezes weaving through the tall herbage.

TRANSPORTATION

Additional Internet Information
http://www.catalina.com/gettingto.html
http://www.catalina.com/airport.html
http://www.catalina.com/directions.html
http://www.catalina.com/express.html
http://www.catalina.com/helicopter.html

Santa Catalina Island has for years attracted tourists because of its romantic and seclusive qualities. Even as far back as the George Shatto era, guests would tolerate long steamship rides across the channel and endure a weekend living in tents, simply to enjoy the island's peaceful, uninterrupted bliss. Today, much has changed in the way of transportation. Boats are not only faster, but more seaworthy and able to hold many passengers. Moreover, the era of flight has come to Catalina as well; helicopters and private planes land here daily. In this section we'll discuss those transportation services that cater to Catalina Island travel. We will also address key topics of private transit.

Many people journey to Catalina to see neat marine life during the submarine tours and the glass bottom boat tours. This is a juvenile garibaldi.

Public Transportation by Sea

Catalina Channel Express

In service since:	1981
Number of vessels in fleet:	8
Size of vessels:	Range from 60 to 95 feet
Passenger capacity:	Up to 302
Departure port/s:	San Pedro, Long Beach, and Dana Point
Destination/s:	Avalon and Two Harbors
Number of daily crossings:	30 (peak season)
Crossing time:	45 minutes to 1½ hours

Reservation Information:
- From the San Pedro Terminal:
  - Phone: (800) 481-3470
  - Address: Catalina Terminal, Berth 95, San Pedro
- From the Long Beach Terminal:
  - Phone: (800) 481-3470
  - Address: 1046 Queensway Hwy., Long Beach (At the Queen Mary)
- From the Dana Point Terminal:
  - Phone: (800) 481-3470
  - Address: 34675 Golden Lantern, Dana Point

Boat features: Unique hull and propulsion attributes help the fleet withstand swell and surface chop activity • Airline-style seating • Main and upper level decks • Snack bar and cocktail service • Exclusive Captain's Lounge for groups

Baggage guidelines: Luggage limited to 2 bags, each no more than 70 pounds—applies to those bringing scuba gear as well • Extra baggage loaded at captain's discretion • An additional carry-on is permitted if it fits underneath your seat • Scuba gear is permitted • One scuba tank per person • Additional charges incurred if transporting surfboards or bikes, space permitting • Pets are allowed but must be restrained in animal carriers or muzzled and leashed • Special baggage requests should be approved well before your trip.

Cross Channel Carrier Reservations Information

Make transportation reservations at least two weeks in advance, particularly during April through October when tourism picks up. Passengers should call the reservation's operator one or two days before their departure to confirm bookings. Also, passengers are highly encouraged to show up at least 30 minutes prior to departure time. If highway traffic is a concern, allow enough time so that you still reach the terminal early. If you push the time limits and show up at the terminal late, it is possible the carrier will have sold your seat to a standby. On the other hand, those seeking a last minute reservation can check in at the terminal reservation desk and purchase canceled or "no-show" seats if they are available.

Catalina Cruises

In service since:	1972
Number of vessels in fleet:	5
Size of vessels:	3 at 135' • 1 at 65' • 1 at 144'
Passenger capacity:	3 at 700 • 1 at 110 • 1 at 450
Departure Port/s:	Long Beach
Destination/s:	Avalon and Two Harbors
Number of daily crossings:	5 (peak season)
Crossing time:	55 minutes to 2 Hours

Reservation information:
  Long Beach Terminal:
    Phone: (800) 228-2546
    Address: 320 Golden Shore Bl.
    Downtown Long Beach

Boat features: Triple deck design • Spacious decks • Secured benches on the outside decks • Cafe-style booths in the cabins • Two snack and cocktail bars

Baggage guidelines: Passengers must be able to carry their own luggage on and off the boat in one trip • Scuba tanks and weight belts are stored at the stern of the boat • One scuba tank per person • Luggage is stored on the floor in the center of the main deck • There is an additional charge to transport surfboards or bikes, space permitting • Pets are allowed, but must be restrained in animal carriers or muzzled and leashed • Special baggage requests should be approved well before your trip

Using Your Own Boat for Transportation

For a fee, boat owners have the option of mooring in Avalon, Two Harbors, or any other anchorage at Catalina. Rates are payable by the day and vary depending on vessel size. However, the harbor patrol does not accept reservations; mooring use is on a first come, first served basis.

Additionally, most moorings at Catalina are privately owned. Proprietors are required to give harbor authorities 12 hours advanced notification of their arrival. The Harbor Master will then assure the mooring is available when the owner shows up the next day. Anyone tied to that particular spot are reassigned to another. If additional mooring space is not available, boat owners must anchor for the duration of their stay.

Catalina Passenger Service

In service since:	1964
Number of vessels in fleet:	1
Size of vessel:	118 feet
Passenger capacity:	500
Departure port/s:	Newport Beach
Destination/s:	Avalon
Number of daily crossings:	1
Crossing time:	1¼ hour
Reservation information:	

    Phone: (949) 673-5245
    Address: 400 Main St., Balboa, 92661

Boat features: Catamaran design stabilizes the vessel during channel crossings • 40 foot beam provides ample space to roam about • Triple deck design • Upper level sun deck with bench seating • Full service cocktail and snack lounge • Large stateroom available for groups

Baggage guidelines: Each passenger must be able to hand carry their luggage on and off the boat • Two bags up to 50 pounds each permitted • Extra baggage is loaded at the discretion of the captain • An additional carry-on is allowed as long as it fits underneath your seat • Some limitations on scuba gear apply • There is an additional charge to transport bikes, space permitting

Those with private boats can visit Catalina and obtain a mooring for the duration of their stay. Sometimes, Avalon Bay becomes very crowded with boats during summer weekends.

Catalina Explorer

In service since:	1997
Number of vessels in fleet:	1
Size of vessel:	75 feet
Passenger capacity:	149
Departure port/s:	Dana Point
Destination/s:	Avalon
Number of daily crossings:	1
Crossing time:	1½ hours

Reservation information:
Phone: (877) 4 Dana Point
Address: 34671 Puerto Place
(Dana Point Shipyard parking Lot)

Boat features: High-Speed triple engine Vessel • 20' beam • Double deck design • Upper level sun deck with ample seating • Full service cocktail and snack lounge • Special charter options

Baggage guidelines: Liberal baggage policy • Extra baggage is loaded at the discretion of the captain • Some limitations on scuba gear apply • There is an additional charge to transport bikes, space permitting • Pets allowed, but must be muzzled and leashed, or in an animal carrier

Obtaining a Mooring in Avalon Bay, Descanso Bay and Hamilton Cove

Boaters arriving in Avalon are encouraged to hold at the entrance of the harbor until approached by the harbor patrol. If patrol vessels are nowhere in sight, boaters can summon them on VHF channel 12, 24-hours a day. The harbor master will then assign the boating party to a mooring in Avalon, Descanso Bay, or Hamilton Cove, provided one is available.

Obtaining a Mooring in Two Harbors and all other Non-Avalon Mooring Sites

Visitors should hold at the harbor entrance until approached by the harbor patrol. If visual contact is ineffective, boaters can reach harbor personnel on VHF channel 9 by asking for the Catalina Harbor Department. If mooring space is unavailable, boaters may request a mooring at another cove location or anchor outside the moorings.

Visitor's Assistance

Catalina's boating crowd is offered many important services. The following information outlines these key services:

Dinghy Docks

Dinghy docks are accessible in Avalon and Two Harbors. Because these landing platforms are relatively small, harbor authorities do not permit boaters to dock dinghies that are more than 13 feet (4 m) in length. To guard against theft, boaters should secure their small boats with a locking cable or chain. The engine should also have some kind of security mechanism. Dinghies are not to be left on the dock more than 72 hours. Island authorities assume no liability for theft or damage; using the dinghy docks is done at your own risk.

Shore boats

Shore boats shuttle boaters to and from shore. Boaters are charged an "each way" fee. To have a shore boat come to your vessel for passenger pickup, call VHF channel 9 and ask for Avalon or Isthmus shore boat, depending on your harbor location. When they respond, give them your mooring number and the cove from which you are calling.

Dinghy docks can congest easily. To maintain maximum space, no dinghies more than 13 feet are permitted at the docks.

Shore boats are used to shuttle passengers to and from shore.

Marine Fuel Docks

Two fuel docks provide gas, diesel fuel, water and snacks.

In Avalon: At the Casino Point dock, (310) 510-0046.

In Two Harbors: Located on the pier, (310) 510-0303.

Boat Parts

Boaters able to make their own repairs but need to obtain parts can do so at Avalon's Sherrill Marine (310-510-1610). Joe's Rent-A-Boat, (310-510-0455) located on the green Pleasure Pier, is an authorized Johnson/ Evinrude repair depot, but works on a variety of other brand name outboard engines as well.

Marine Mechanic

Several marine mechanics at Catalina are available to provide emergency service to boaters who need mechanical assistance. Boaters requesting this service should call the following VHF channels and ask for "marine repair."

In Avalon Only: Channel 16   *Locations other than Avalon:* Channel 9

Vessel Assist

Boaters who become stranded due to mechanical problems can call **Avalon Harbor Department on VHF channel 12** or **Isthmus Harbor Department at VHF channel 9** for a tow. However, if your position is too far from either town, call **"Vessel Assist" on VHF channel 16** for assistance. Vessel Assist may also be contacted by calling **(310) 510-1610.** Fees vary depending on how far the rescue boat must travel and whether you carry current Vessel Assistant insurance.

Special Diving Services

It is not uncommon for boaters to experience unexpected problems while anchored or moored in Avalon or Two Harbors. The nature of these quandaries might include lost props, wallets fumbled overboard or expensive fishing rods and reels knocked into the water. What do you do if you want these back? There are several island marine services that can help:

In Avalon

Avalon Mooring and Diving Service:	(310) 510-0779 or VHF Ch. 12
Argo Diving Service:	(310) 510-2208 or VHF Ch. 8

All other areas

Catalina Mooring Service:	(310) 510-0303 or VHF Ch. 9

Rules for Boaters

Boaters wishing to anchor or moor at Catalina must comply with the following guidelines:

1. Mooring sites are NO-DISCHARGE areas. Whether it is treated or not, releasing sewage is unlawful. Free use of PUMP-A-HEADS is available at the Avalon dock. The public rest room at Two Harbors has disposal facilities for Porta-Potties.
2. Do not throw trash into the water! Service boats make trash pick ups in Avalon daily during summer months and on weekends in the wintertime. When service boats are not convenient, large trash containers are available at the docks for disposal of refuse.
3. To avoid irritating nearby boaters, skippers must shut down generators from 10:00 p.m. to 7:00 a.m. daily.
4. Anchoring within the confines of Avalon Bay is prohibited. Boaters who choose to anchor must do so outside the breakwater, west of the Casino. At all other mooring sites, boaters must remain outside the mooring perimeter to anchor. Anchoring is done at your own risk.
5. Though no reservations are accepted, boaters can obtain current information about mooring availability by calling one of the following numbers:
In Avalon:
Avalon Harbor Department (310-510-0535)
In Two Harbors and all other mooring sites:
Catalina Harbor Department (310-510-2683)

Dealing With Motion Sickness

The excitement of traveling to Catalina begins once your shuttle leaves port, but traveling across the channel can be very uncomfortable for passengers who are prone to motion sickness. Cross channel passengers should take precautions if this fits their profile. Motion sickness medication is available over-the-counter in most drug stores.

Passengers taking non prescribed motion sickness medication should follow directions on the package carefully. Some medications require they be taken a couple of hours before boarding a boat or airplane. Individuals often wait until they are feeling queasy and turning green before taking their medication, but by this time it is too late and they must endure the suffering. If over-the-counter medications do not work well for you, more effective measures are available through a physician.

In the event one becomes ill, motion sickness containers are available on each cross channel carrier. The restrooms are also sometimes used, but for sanitary purposes operation owners prefer the prior method. As a free service, all vessels in each fleet supply soda crackers (Saltine crackers, for example) to help settle your stomach during bouts of nausea.

Though some people are more susceptible to motion sickness than others, there are a few guidelines to follow that may help to reduce its severity.

1.   Eat a light meal before departure time. A little food in the stomach may actually prevent sea sickness. Do not eat greasy foods such as fried eggs or chile. Meals of this sort often augment sea sickness. Passengers feeling nauseous should consider sipping some 7-UP, which may help settle their stomachs.

2.   Get ample rest the night before your departure. Individuals have reported that a good night's sleep helped prevent motion sickness symptoms the next day. Other times when sleep was minimal, these same individuals became ill.

3.   Once on the boat, get some fresh air. Stale cabin air can intensify the effect of motion sickness.

4.   Avoid standing near the stern of the boat close to the engine's exhaust. The pungent smell of diesel or gas fumes frequently amplifies motion sickness symptoms.

5.   When the seas are rough, try to stay in an area near the centerline of the boat where swaying is minimal. Also, stay off upper level decks to avoid intensified teeter-totter effects.

Sea sickness typically subsides after setting foot on solid ground. What might persist for some individuals is the feeling of still being on a boat, resulting in an occasional wobbling of the knees. In a few hours, affected individuals will gain back their land-legs and recover fully.

Public Transportation by Air

Only two air transport services cater to Santa Catalina Island travel: **Island Express**, stationed in both Long Beach and San Pedro, and **Catalina Vegas Airlines** out of San Diego. The following is a brief overview of each service along with helpful booking information and baggage guidelines.

Island Express

In Service Since:	1982
Passenger Capacity:	6 (or 850 lbs.)
Departure Port/s:	Long Beach and San Pedro
Destination/s:	Avalon
Number of Daily Crossings:	Hourly on demand
Crossing Time:	15 minutes
Landing Site:	Pebbly Beach Helipad, near Avalon

Reservation Information:
From San Pedro:
Phone: 1-800-2-AVALON
Address: Catalina Terminal, Berth 95 & 96, San Pedro
From Long Beach:
Phone: 1-800-2-AVALON
Address: 900 Queensway Dr., Long Beach

Baggage guidelines: Weight and space limitations are critical concerns on a helicopter. If traveling weight and passenger capacity is minimal, pilots may be lenient with their baggage restrictions. However, company policy dictates a 25-pound maximum luggage allowance per passenger. After that, if adequate space and weight allowance remains, there is a small per pound charge for excess baggage.
Scuba tanks are not allowed on flights unless they are first emptied. Scuba gear is welcome, but Island Express strongly encourages divers to rent gear from one of Catalina's dive shops.

Catalina–Vegas Airline

In service since:	1978
Passenger capacity:	2
Departure Port/s:	Montgomery Field, San Diego
Destination/s:	Airport in the Sky
Number of daily crossings:	Daily on demand
Crossing time:	30 minutes
Landing Site:	Airport in the Sky

Reservation Information
Phone: 1-800-339-0FLY
Address: 3760 Glen Curtis Rd., Montgomery Field, San Diego

Baggage guidelines: Unfortunately, baggage space is extremely limited. There is inadequate space to store scuba gear, pets or large bags. Catalina-Vegas guidelines dictate that passengers bring one, maybe two, small overnight bags only.

Private Transportation by Air

Airport In The Sky

Private pilots may land their planes at Catalina's Airport-in-the-Sky. The airport's 3,250 foot (990 m) runway can accommodate most moderately sized airplanes, including Lear jets and other comparable aircraft. Pilots are charged a $5 landing fee, and if you choose to spend more than one consecutive day on the island, an additional $5 per night tie-down fee is charged. Fees must be paid in advance. The airport is open seven

Private planes have landed at Catalina's airport since 1959.

days a week. During the months of April through October it is open from 8:00 a.m. to 7:00 p.m.. The rest of the year it operates from 8:00 a.m. to 5:00 p.m..

To speak directly with airport operations, call (310) 510-0143. For current weather information call the airport's toll free weather report at 1-800-255-8700 or call (310) 510-9641 24 hours a day.

Getting to Town Once You Land

To Avalon from the Helipad: Before your departure, let the pilot know you need a taxi. They will then radio ahead to Avalon's taxi service, which will subsequently be at the helipad upon your arrival. Taxi fees are $5 to $7.

To Two Harbors from the Helipad: Inform the pilot upon your mainland departure that you would like a taxi to meet you at the helipad. Have the taxi driver take you to the "Plaza," where the Safari Bus Company meets passengers seeking transportation to Two Harbors. Making reservations with Safari Bus Company (310-510-0303) prior to your mainland departure is important.

To Avalon From the Airport
The airport offers shuttle service to and from Avalon year-round. Guests are strongly encouraged to book a shuttle seat well before their mainland departure. Do not wait until arrival at the airport to book a space. Although there are several daily shuttle pickups, they often fill quickly. You may end up sitting at the airport until the next scheduled shuttle arrives. To book a seat, call the airport at (310) 510-0143.

To Two Harbors From the Airport
The Safari Bus Company provides year-round shuttle service between the airport and Two Harbors. Because shuttle schedules vary with the season, visitors should obtain a current routing schedule prior to departing the mainland. Safari Bus Company encourages guests to make shuttle bookings one–two weeks before mainland departure.

Catalina Taxi Services
In Avalon

Avalon has two local transportation services catering to the tourist market. Below lists and describes these operations.

Catalina Transportation Services (CTS)   (310) 510-0025

Catalina Transportation Service maintains a fleet of ten vans, like the ones pictured here.

Catalina Transportation Services, also known as Catalina Cab Company, is Avalon's only taxi operation. Located on Crescent Street across from Antonio's Pizzeria, CTS meets every arriving cross channel carrier to serve disembarking passengers. No reservations are required; CTS continually circulates their fleet of vans until no more passengers are waiting for a ride. Reasonable fees apply unless you are staying at a CTS contracted hotel, then it's free.

General taxi service is available as well, but must be coordinated through the CTS dispatcher. Visitors can either call or show up at the main booth to obtain a taxi, provided one is available. A customer may also request an advanced reservation pick up. In this case, CTS personnel will pick you up according to your reserved time slot. Fees vary with destination and passenger loads. Catalina Transportation Service is also available for private charter.

Avalon Baggage Services (ABS)   (310) 510-2116

Avalon Baggage Service provides gear and luggage transportation for groups or individuals with large loads of freight, such as scuba diving groups. ABS provides baggage transportation assistance to every cross channel transport arriving at the mole. Anyone stepping off the cross channel carriers can utilize ABS's services without prior arrangements. Fees are contingent on load capacity; if you are staying at an ABS contracted hotel, baggage service is complimentary.

Avalon Baggage Service is a vital link between diving clientele and island diving operations; they provide needed transportation service for groups with large baggage loads, such as those associated with divers.

ABS also delivers door to door. This is ideal for scuba divers wishing to have gear delivered to and from their hotel to the Underwater Park, or bands needing music equipment transported to a night club, for example. You can coordinate baggage service by calling the ABS dispatcher or by asking your hotel operator to make arrangements for you.

ABS Daily Storage Facility

Though some hotels provide temporary baggage storage for guests who have checked out, many are unable to offer this option. The alternative is to use the Avalon Baggage storage service located near the Cabrillo Mole terminal. Here, visitors can safely store dive gear, suitcases and other equipment until their cross-channel transport departs. Pay lockers are available if your baggage load is small or you can check your bags in with a resident ABS employee, who will then tag them and provide a claim ticket for each checked piece.

When reclaiming baggage, customers must present their claim tickets at the check stand; misplaced vouchers create problems when attempting to retrieve baggage. Storage fees rarely exceed $5 for the day. No overnight storage is allowed.

In Two Harbors

Safari Bus Company   (310) 510-0303

The Safari Bus Company provides transportation service between the airport, Avalon and Two Harbors, but also stops at a variety of sites along the way. The vans are spacious and hold 10 or more people, including their luggage. Destination schedules vary throughout the year, so it's recommended that tourists call for a current shuttle agenda.

In addition, guests are encouraged to make shuttle reservations at least 24 hours before their mainland departure. The shuttles might be full and passengers may have to wait an hour or more before the next available van arrives. Island guests requesting special transportation or charter service can hire a Safari van at an hourly rate.

Sea Transportation Services (Quick Reference)

Name	Departure Port	Phone Number	Address	Crossing Time	Destination	Page
Catalina Express	San Pedro	(310) 519-1212	Catalina Terminal Berth 95 San Pedro	1 to 1½ Hours	Avalon Two Harbors	36
Catalina Express	Long Beach	(310) 519-1212	1046 Queensway Hwy. Long Beach	1 Hour	Avalon Two Harbors	36
Catalina Express	Dana Point	(310) 519-1212	34675 Golden Lantern Dana Point	1½ Hours	Avalon Two Harbors	36
Catalina Cruises	Long Beach	(800) 228-2546	320 Golden Shore Blvd. Long Beach	2 Hours	Avalon Two Harbors	37
Catalina Passenger Service	Newport Beach	(714) 673-5245	400 Main St. Balboa	1¼ Hours	Avalon	38
Catalina Explorer	Dana Point	(877) 4-Dana Point	34671 Puerto Place Dana Point	1½ Hours	Avalon	39

Key Points Review of Sea Transportation

- Secure a departure and arrival schedule from the specific operator
- Inquire about baggage limitations (weight, size, type of baggage, etc.) well in advance of your trip
- Make reservations at least two weeks in advance
- Pack efficiently
- Show up at the departure terminal at least 30 minutes early
- Prepare for motion sickness if susceptible

Island Services (Quick Reference)

Name of Service	Phone Number	Description of Services	Page
Airport in the Sky	(310) 510-0143	Airport operations Cross-island Shuttle booking	44
Airport in the sky weather report	(800) 255-8700 or (310) 510-9641	Weather report for landing conditions	44
Argo Diving Service	(310) 510-2208 (VHF Ch. 8)	Mooring Maintenance and Search & Salvage in Avalon	41
Avalon Baggage Service	(310) 510-2116	Baggage & Equipment transportation in Avalon	46
Avalon Harbor Department	(310) 510-0535	Mooring availability in Avalon • Boating regulations • Emergencies	41
Avalon Mooring & Diving Service	(310) 510-0779 (VHF Ch. 12)	Mooring maintenance and Search & Salvage in Avalon	41
Catalina Mooring Service	(310) 510-0303 (VHF Ch. 9)	Mooring maintenance and Search & Salvage in Two Harbors	41
Catalina Transportation Service	(310) 510-0025	Taxi service to entire island	45
Catalina Vegas Airlines	(800) 339-0FLY	Airplane service to Catalina's airport	44
Island Express	(800) 2AVALON	Helicopter service to Pebbly Beach near Avalon	43
Isthmus Harbor Department	(310) 510-2683	Mooring availability in Isthmus • Boating regulations • Emergencies	41
Joe's Rent-A-Boat	(310) 510-0455	Outboard engine repair	40
Marine fuel dock at Casino Point	(310) 510-0046	Gas · Diesel · Water	40
Marine fuel dock at Two Harbors	(310) 510-0303	Gas · Diesel · Water	40
Safari Bus Company	(310) 510-0303	Shuttle service	47
Sherrill Marine	(310) 510-1610	Boat parts · Marine engine repair	40
Vessel Assist	(310) 510-1610 (VHF Ch. 16)	Emergency service for stranded boaters	41

HOTELS

Additional Internet Information
http//www.catalina.com/lodging.html#hotels
http//www.catalina.com/lodging.html#availability
http//www.catalina.com/twoharbors/index.html

Hotel Descriptions

In one square mile, Avalon has more than 30 hotels from which to choose; selecting one depends on your lodging taste. As a whole, the hotels in this small city accommodate the entire tourist market by providing a selection from economical to extravagant lodging, ranging from $35 to $550 per night. The less expensive hotels typically maintain original structure and lore, offering a straight forward, no frills approach to lodging. Other mid to high end establishments have been gutted and refurbished with modern amenities, such as fireplaces and whirlpool hot tubs to emphasize a finer class of living.

Within the mix of lodging options are romantic getaways, bed and breakfast establishments, hotels of historical significance, hillside mansions, share-bath bungalows, and ocean front resorts. The fun is choosing a hotel that is right for you.

Considerations when Selecting a Hotel

Ocean View: Not all hotels at Catalina have ocean views, and some that claim they do are often referring to a partial view. If a clear panorama of the bay is preferred, then guests should expressly petition it when making hotel reservations. Otherwise, a neighboring building may be your scenery. The number of rooms with an ocean view is depicted in the individual hotel descriptions as "Rooms W/OV" and in the quick reference at the end of this chapter.

Restrooms: A few hotels are "share-bath," meaning that the entire floor must share a common washroom facility, or adjoining rooms must share a single rest room. These hotels are typically rustic in their luxuries, but offer more pleasing rates. Be sure to ask specifically about rest room facilities if a share bath arrangement is unacceptable.

Amenities: Many hotels are equipped with varying amenities such as in room fireplaces and hot tubs. However, these features may only be available in selected rooms. Do not assume your room will come "amenity ready." Explore whether the specific room you're being quoted has the advertised features you desire.

Rates: Hotel rates vary depending on how modern the facility is, what amenities are provided, how much of an ocean view the room has, the location of the building and its historical significance. Rates also fluctuate with the seasons. Though specific prices are not listed, each hotel is categorized based on their peak season, weekend rates. Midweek and winter rates are considerably lower. Keep in mind that most hotels offer a variety of views and amenity choices, which may broaden their pricing scheme significantly.

For example, a hotel might have a room available for $200 a night that has a complete ocean view, in room refrigerator, fireplace and whirlpool hot tub. In the same hotel might be a room offered for $80 a night; however, it lacks the ocean view and the other aforementioned amenities. Therefore, the "rate category" dictated for each hotel may reflect more than one pricing classification.

Package Rates: Many island hotels offer special rate packages that may save their guests money. A package example might include cross-channel transportation, two tours and two nights accommodations. Compared to purchasing the same options separately, customers may save up to 20 percent. If you are interested in booking a package arrangement, make sure to mention it when querying a hotel operator.

Creating your own weekend package: A convenient feature most hotels tout is the option for guests to devise their own packages. This generally includes cross-channel transportation, lodging, and any combination of tours and activities desired. Though no cost reduction is generally attributed, it is comforting to know that experienced hotel operators are there to help, extending to their customers a savings of time, frustration and guaranteed space.

Booking a Room: Because wintertime crowds are characteristically small, guests can usually reserve a room with a one week notification. However, crowds increase significantly from April through October, so you should make reservations well before your anticipated arrival date. Request that a booking confirmation be sent to you. Make a verbal confirmation several days prior to your trip to ensure your booking has not been lost.

Minimum stay policy: During winter most Catalina hotels honor one night stays on weekdays and weekends. However, policies change during the peak season. Most hotels implement a two night "minimum stay" policy during the weekends (Fridays, Saturdays and Sundays).

Cancellation policy: Cancellation policies can be very severe and unpleasant if you are unaware of the cost consequences. To minimize penalties, it is important to know about the hotel's present cancellation policy before booking a room. Pets: By ordinance of the city of Avalon municipal code, pets are not allowed in any lodging establishment.

Loud noise: The city of Avalon has a 10:30 p.m. noise abatement policy in which all hotel guests must refrain from becoming so loud that it disturbs other hotel guests. Local authorities will deal with reported disturbances accordingly.

Scuba Amenities: Divers bringing scuba equipment to Catalina should first make sure that the hotel they are querying has facilities to store bulk, wet items. Many lack storage space, and prohibit divers from keeping gear in the rooms. These hotels are identified in the hotel descriptions and in the quick reference at the end of this chapter. Realistically, only about a dozen hotels have amenities that are actually intended for diving gear. Commonly, hotel personnel claiming to have scuba amenities may be referring to a janitorial closet and garden hose. Though this might work for individual divers, it could be catastrophic for larger groups. To avoid potential conflicts, make sure your hotel has facilities that accommodate your requirements. There are three main lodging factors to consider if bringing diving gear to Catalina Island:

Storage lockers: Ask specifically if gear storage lockers are available to support the number of divers in your group. Those hotels that provide individual storage lockers generally require divers to supply their own locks. Some hotels put all gear in one big room; make sure they lock it at night.

Rinsing facilities: Some hotels catering to divers lack fresh water rinsing facilities, while others are fully equipped for the chore. Divers choosing to clean dive equipment after each day of diving should first ensure the hotel provides rinsing provisions.

Shuttle service: Investigate whether your chosen hotel provides complimentary shuttle service to and from Casino Point or the Cabrillo Mole boat dock. If they do, Avalon Baggage Service or a hotel van will meet your group at the hotel accordingly to transport your gear. Otherwise, hotel operators can arrange gear transportation through Avalon Baggage Service for a nominal fee.

If arriving by private boat, arrangements to have your gear picked up and transported to your island destination can be made by calling Avalon Baggage Service at (310) 510-2888 or (310) 510-2116.

Hotel Descriptions

Following are brief descriptions of the lodging options available on Catalina Island. The intention of this section is to provide helpful information that is likely to aid in your hotel selection process.

Hotels in Avalon

Atwater Hotel

Built:	1920; remodeled in 1996
Map Location:	1
Motif:	Early Catalina
No. of Rooms:	100
Rooms w/Ocean View:	25
Features:	Private baths • Cable T.V. • Budget prices • Unsecured storage for scuba gear • Some in-room refrigerators & microwaves • King size beds in suites • Some wetbars • Jacuzzi tubs • Air conditioning
Address:	125 Sumner Ave. • P.O. Box 737 • Avalon • CA • 90704
Phone Number:	(310) 510-2500 or (800) 626-9602
Rules:	3-day cancellation policy
Rate Category:	Expensive
General Comments:	Atwater's rooms are small but contain adequate furnishings for a comfortable stay. The hotel also has a large storage room for scuba gear, but it remains unlocked at all times. Atwater is closed from November to March, but available for special bookings year-round.

Bay View Hotel

Built:	1928
Map Location:	2
Motif:	Early Catalina
No. of Rooms:	20
Rooms w/Ocean View:	4
Features:	Some private baths • Color cable T.V. • Free continental breakfast • Whirlpool baths in two rooms • King size beds • Large patio area with Jacuzzi and barbeque • Scuba amenities • Diver shuttle service
Address:	124 Whittley Ave • P.O. Box 774 • Avalon • CA • 90704
Phone Number:	(310) 510-7070
Rules:	7-day cancellation policy
Rate Category:	Budget
General Comments:	Bay View is a budget lodging option. Most of the rooms are a share bath arrangement—that is, there is one common washroom facility for men and one for women. This hotel is popular among scuba divers because of its inexpensive rates and full scuba amenities (secured gear lockers, rinse tank, drying racks, etc.).

Buena Vista

Built:	1924
Map Location:	3
Motif:	Basic, no-frills accommodations
No. of Rooms:	10
Rooms w/Ocean View:	1 full • 3 partial
Features:	Color T.V. • Barbecue • Private baths • Small courtyard patio • In room refrigerators • Large rooms
Address:	120 Whittley Ave. • P.O. Box 571 • Avalon • CA • 90704
Phone Number:	(310) 510-0340
Rules:	7-day cancellation policy • No credit cards accepted, only checks and cash
Rate category:	Budget to moderate
General Comments:	Offers exceptionally affordable rates.

Casa Mariquita

Built:	Rebuilt in 1989
Map Location:	4
Motif:	Spanish
No. of Rooms:	22
Rooms w/Ocean View:	4 full • 3 partial
Features:	Color cable T.V. • Barbecue • Complimentary transportation • In room refrigerators • In room phones • Private baths • Two courtyard patios • Limited scuba amenities • Free continental breakfast
Address:	229 Metropole Ave. • P.O. Box 2487 • Avalon • CA • 90704
Phone Number:	(310) 510-1192 or (800) 545-1192
Rules:	No hard or wet gear in rooms • 14-day cancellation policy
Rate category:	Moderate to very expensive
General Comments:	One premier suite has a full kitchen, and two balconies with sweeping views. The other has a full harbor view, private balcony, but no kitchen.

Catalina Beach House

Built:	1912
Map Location:	5
Motif:	Converted flat bottom houseboat
No of Rooms:	23
Rooms w/Ocean View:	2
Features:	Ocean view courtyard patio • Kitchenettes in rooms • Color cable T.V. with VCR • Diver shuttle service • Whirlpool baths • In room refrigerators • Nonsmoking rooms available • In room phones • Scuba amenities • Barbecue • Air and heat • King and queen beds • Video library on premises
Address:	200 Marilla Ave. • P.O. Box 64 • Avalon • CA • 90704
Phone:	(310) 510-1078 or (800) 97-HOTEL
Rules:	No smoking in some rooms • 7-day cancellation policy
Rate category:	Moderate
General Comments:	Catalina Beach House has, in recent years, been completely gutted and refurbished while retaining its 1912 lore. Many units now have connecting rooms for families. The Beach House also provides diving equipment rinse facilities and outlets to store scuba gear.

Catalina Cottages / Hermosa Hotel

Built:	Late 1800s
Map Location:	7
Motif:	Late 1800 history and architecture
No. of Rooms:	56
Rooms w/Ocean View:	None
Features:	Private baths in cottages • Scuba gear storage available • Kitchenettes in cottages • Bungalows
Address:	131 Metropole Ave. • P.O. Box 646 • Avalon • CA • 90704
Phone:	(888) 684-1313
Rules:	No In room guests after 10:00 p.m. • 4-day cancellation policy
Rate category:	Budget to moderate
General Comments:	Catalina Cottages, also known as Hermosa Hotel, offers their guests three types of lodging options:
Cottages:	These units are outfitted with private baths and queen, double or twin beds. Two cottages hold up to eight guests, while the others sleep two to four.
Bungalows and hotel:	These lodging options cost less but are a little more rustic in their living qualities. The hotel is a share bath arrangement and somewhat small. The rooms lack phones, T.V.'s, air conditioning and heat. The bungalows offer the same features except that guests must share one common washroom facility between rooms.

Catalina Canyon (Best Western) Hotel

Built:	1963; more rooms added in 1986
Map Location:	6
Motif:	Romantic, lush garden setting
No. of Rooms:	80
Rooms w/Ocean View:	None • About a half-dozen rooms have canyon views
Features:	Private baths • In room phones • Seasonal continental breakfast • Free shuttle service • Swimming pool, jacuzzi and sauna • Non-smoking rooms available • Air conditioned and heated rooms • Color cable T.V. • Suites available • Scuba Amenities • Restaurant on premises • Day spa
Address:	888 Country Club Dr. • P.O. Box 736 • Avalon • CA • 90704
Phone:	(310) 510-0325 or (800) 253-9361
Rules:	Follow smoking regulations • 3-day cancellation policy
Rate category:	Moderate
General Comments:	The rooms provide luxury living quarters for individuals, groups, and businesses that seek a business-like atmosphere. Catalina Canyon has conference room facilities available for up to 150 people. Guests are also encouraged to dine at the hotel's restaurant, the Canyon Grill, which is open year-round. The hotel is not in close proximity to mainstream Avalon or the water.

Catalina Canyon Best Western hotel is one of a few hotels at Catalina with a swimming pool.

Catalina Island Inn

Built:	1907 • Remodeled in 1985
Map Location:	8
Motif:	Romantic Victorian
No. of Rooms:	36
Rooms w/Ocean View:	10
Features:	Private baths • Heat • In room phones • King and queen beds • Color cable T.V. • Free continental breakfast • Suites • Getaway Packages available
Address:	125 Metropole Ave. • P.O. Box 467 • Avalon • CA • 90704
Phone:	(310) 510-1623
Rules:	3-day cancellation policy
Rate category:	Moderate to expensive
General Comments:	The rooms at Catalina Island Inn have a fresh and sunny decor. The inn itself is conveniently located in the heart of Cricket Alley shopping promenade.

The rooms at Catalina Island Inn are decorated and furnished to epitomize contemporary living. Some of them provide superb views of Avalon Bay.

Catalina Lodge

Built:	1950s
Map Location:	9
Motif:	Basic, family-oriented living
No. of Rooms:	15
Rooms w/Ocean View:	None
Features:	Color cable T.V. • Refrigerators in most rooms • Private baths • Heat • Scuba amenities • Non-smoking rooms available
Address:	235 Sumner Ave. • P.O. Box 1103 • Avalon • CA • 90704
Phone:	(310) 510-1070 or (800) 974-1070
Rules:	7-day cancellation policy
Rate category:	Moderate
General Comments:	Primary clientele includes families and groups. The rooms are plain, but clean and comfortable.

Catherine Hotel

Built:	Early 1900s
Map Location:	10
Motif:	Early 19th century
No. of Rooms:	15
Rooms w/Ocean View:	3
Features:	Color T.V. • Private baths • One non-smoking room • Bar and restaurant on premises • Live weekend entertainment • Scuba amenities
Address:	708 Crescent Ave. • P.O. Box 1638 • Avalon • CA • 90704
Phone Number:	(310) 510-0170
Rules:	14-day cancellation policy
Rate category:	Moderate
General Comments:	Before the owners converted it into a lodging establishment, the white and blue trim Catherine Hotel was originally a large mansion.

Cloud 7 Hotel

Built:	1963
Map Location:	11
Motif:	Victorian
No. of Rooms:	17
Rooms w/Ocean View:	5
Features:	Private baths • Color cable T.V. • Free continental breakfast • Vacation customizing service • Mini refrigerators in rooms • Air conditioning and heat • In room coffee brewer • Queen or double beds • Scuba amenities • Package rates available
Address:	137 Marilla Ave. • P.O. Box 1557 • Avalon • CA • 90704
Phone Number:	(310) 510-0454 or (800) 422-6836
Rules:	6-day cancellation policy
Rate Category:	Moderate
General Comments:	Although built in 1963, Cloud 7 was refurbished in 1988 to include many modern amenities. In addition, gear rinse and storage facilities, with racks to drip dry wet scuba gear, are furnished for diving guests.

Edgewater Hotel

Built:	1900
Map Location:	12
Motif:	Southwestern
No. of Rooms:	8
Rooms w/Ocean View:	2
Features:	Private baths • Color cable T.V. with VCR • Fireplaces • Free continental breakfast • Courtyard • Whirlpool tubs in suites • Scuba amenities • Two multiple room suites with ocean views • In room refrigerators
Address:	415 Crescent Ave. • P.O. Box 647 • Avalon • CA • 90704
Phone Number:	(310) 510-0347 or (800) 89-HOTEL
Rules:	Electrical shut down of the jacuzzi at 10:30 p.m. • 10-day cancellation policy • No smoking policy in rooms
Rate Category:	Expensive to very expensive
General Comments:	In 1989, the hotel was completely gutted and refurbished to include deluxe rooms and large, luxurious suites.

El Terado Terrace

Built:	1972
Map Location:	13
Motif:	Modern California
No. of Rooms:	18
Rooms w/Ocean View:	6
Features:	Color cable T.V. • Private baths • Hot tub • Kitchens or wet bars • Barbecues • Group rates • Sun deck • Suites
Address:	230 Marilla Ave. • P.O. Box 1295 • Avalon • CA • 90704
Phone:	(310) 510-0831 or (800) 540-0139
Rules:	5-day cancellation policy
Rate category:	Budget to expensive
General Comments:	El Terado Terrace offers town home-style accommodations, or single room alternatives. Some two-story town homes can accommodate groups of six, making it an economical lodging option. Guests may also choose from standard, deluxe and mini suites.

Hotel Catalina

Built:	1915
Map Location:	15
Motif:	Victorian
No. of Rooms:	32
Rooms w/Ocean View:	10
Features:	Color cable T.V. • Spa • Honeymoon cottages • Barbecue • Private baths • Free morning coffee • Sun patio • Scuba amenities
Address:	129 Whittley Ave. • P.O. Box 365 • Avalon • CA • 90704
Phone Number:	(310) 510-0027
Rules:	5-day cancellation policy
Rate category:	Moderate
General Comments:	Hotel Catalina is one of the island's numerous landmarks, originally built in 1892, but reconstructed after fire destroyed it in 1915. In addition to the brightly decorated rooms, there are large honeymoon and family cottages available, some of which have kitchens. Because Hotel Catalina is perched atop a hillside, visitors will enjoy a spectacular view of Avalon Bay from the balustrade railing balconies.

Glenmore Plaza Hotel

Built:	1892
Map Location:	14
Motif:	Early California – touch of romance
No. of Rooms:	50
Rooms w/Ocean View:	3 full • 6 partial
Features:	Color T.V. • Whirlpool tubs • Air conditioning and heat • Color cable T.V. • Barbecue • Free continental breakfast • Free shuttle service • Elaborate suites
Address:	120 Sumner Ave. • Avalon • CA • 90704
Phone:	(310) 510-0017 or (800) 4-CATALINA
Rules:	7-day cancellation policy
Rate category:	Expensive
General Comments:	The completely renovated Glenmore Plaza Hotel is the oldest surviving hotel on Catalina and the second oldest in all of California. It has attracted many world renowned notables such as Clark Gable, Teddy Roosevelt, and Amelia Earhart. The main appeal of the hotel is the Clark Gable suite, which entertains a circular cupola bedroom with a 360-degree panorama. A spiral staircase leads down to its spacious living area, where visitors can enjoy its elaborate surroundings.

The Clark Gable Suite at Glenmore Plaza hotel is among the most extravagant suites at Catalina.

Hotel Mac Rae

Built:	1920
Map Location:	16
Motif:	Mediterranean
No. of Rooms:	24
Rooms w/Ocean View:	4
Features:	Private baths • Color cable T.V. with VCR • Heat • Complimentary beach towels • Private guest courtyard • Vacation customizing service • Free continental breakfast • Scuba amenities • Non-smoking rooms available
Address:	409 Crescent Ave. • P.O. Box 275 • Avalon • CA • 90704
Phone Number:	(310) 510-2121 or (800) 698-2266
Rules:	6-day cancellation policy
Rate category:	Moderate to expensive
General Comments:	Though Hotel Mac Rae was built in 1920, it went through a dynamic refurbishing project in 1992 and now contains many modern conventions, with no two rooms decorated the same. The hotel is one of Avalon's few beach front lodging enterprises.

Hotel St. Lauren

Built:	1987
Map Location:	18
Motif:	Victorian
No. of Rooms:	42
Rooms w/Ocean View:	3
Features:	Elevator • Color cable T.V. • Ocean view rooms • Conference room facilities • In room phones • Sixth floor rooftop patio • Some whirlpool tubs • Private balconies
Address:	231 Beacon St. • P.O. Box 497 • Avalon • CA • 90704
Phone Number:	(310) 510-2299
Rules:	7-day cancellation policy
Rate category:	Moderate to expensive
General Comments:	The large rooms are outfitted with exquisite rosewood furniture, while the bathrooms are beautifully tiled and brass-fixtured. In addition, owners have installed an elevator as a convenience for hotel guests. On the sixth floor is a rooftop patio with a magnificent view of Avalon and the ocean, which guests use to relax and escape the crowds. Hotel St. Lauren is a recipient of the AAA three-diamond award.

Hotel Metropole

Built:	1990
Map Location:	17
Motif:	Catalina Renaissance
No. of Rooms:	47
Rooms w/Ocean View:	6
Features:	Whirlpool jacuzzi • Private suites • Stocked refrigerators • Free continental breakfast • Private balconies • Direct dial phones • Some fireplaces • Some private In room spas • Conference room facilities • Courtyard
Address:	2025 Crescent Ave. • P.O. Box 1900 • Avalon • CA • 90704
Phone Number:	(310) 510-1884 or (800) 541-8528
Rules:	No smoking in any rooms • 3-day cancellation policy
Rate category:	Moderate to very expensive
General Comments:	Hotel Metropole is a luxurious retreat with an emphasis on upper class living. The rooms are furnished with rich fruitwood furnishings and other custom features that exemplify quality living. On the fourth floor overlooking beautiful Avalon Bay is a whirlpool hot tub for hotel guests to enjoy.

One of Catalina's newest, and most elegant, lodging choices is Hotel Metropole. Guests staying here can enjoy the comfort of an in-room whirlpool hot tub, a fireplace and mini refrigerator stocked with lots of goodies.

Hotel Villa Portofino

Built:	1960
Map Location:	19
Motif:	European
No of Rooms:	34
Rooms w/Ocean View:	3 full • 2 partial
Features:	Private baths • Heated rooms • Large suites • Whirlpools baths in some rooms • Ocean viewing deck • On-premises restaurant • Color cable T.V. • Kitchenettes in suites
Address:	111 Crescent Ave. • P.O. Box 127 • Avalon • CA • 90704
Phone Number:	(310) 510-0555 or (800) 34-OCEAN
Rules:	3-day cancellation policy
Rate category:	Moderate to expensive
General Comments:	All rooms at Hotel Villa Portofino are elegantly blessed with European style and luxury, perfect for honeymoons and romantic getaways. There is an exquisite Italian dining lounge on the main floor of the hotel called Villa Portofino Restorante, where sumptuous Northern Italian cuisine is served. Recipient of the AAA Three-Diamond award.

Hotel Vincentes

Built:	1978
Map Location:	20
Motif:	Mediterranean
No. of Rooms:	12
Rooms w/Ocean View:	2
Features:	Private baths • King beds • In room refrigerators • In room coffee makers • 1000 sq/ft rooms • Heated • Color cable T.V. with VCR • Suites with ocean view terraces • Kitchen area with wet bar and microwave in suites • All nonsmoking rooms • Limited scuba amenities
Address:	108 Marilla Ave. • P.O. Box 187 • Avalon • CA • 90704
Phone Number:	(310) 510-1115
Rules:	Smoking regulations • 10-day cancellation policy
Rate category:	Moderate to very expensive
General Comments:	Hotel Vincentes' clientele consists primarily of honeymooners or those celebrating a birthday or anniversary. Many couples are attracted to the huge, 1,000 square foot suites offered by the hotel. AAA approved hotel.

Hotel Vista Del Mar

Built:	Early 1900s
Map Location:	21
Motif:	Mediterranean
No. of Rooms:	15
Rooms w/Ocean View:	2
Features:	Jacuzzis • Color cable T.V. • Wet bars • Free continental breakfast • Special rate packages • Garden atrium courtyard • Fireplaces • In room phones • Ocean view suites • Robes and like items provided • All non-smoking rooms
Address:	417 Crescent Ave. • P.O. Box 1979 • Avalon • CA • 90704
Phone Number:	(310) 510-1452
Rules:	No smoking in rooms • 5-day cancellation policy
Rate category:	Moderate to very expensive
General Comments:	Hotel Vista Del Mar is a beautiful hotel thoroughly remodeled as a romantic getaway in 1988. It offers luxury accommodations and amenities such as complimentary bath robes and hair dryers. The building surrounds a beautiful garden atrium and includes a 165 gallon, semi-spherical, tropical fish tank. The hotel is a AAA, Three-Star rated operation.

La Paloma Cottages / Las Flores

Built:	1920s
Map Location:	23
Motif:	New Orleans
No. of Rooms:	20
Rooms w/Ocean View:	5
Features:	Private baths • Barbecue • Double whirlpool baths in Las Flores rooms • Air conditioning in Las Flores rooms • VCR in Las Flores rooms • Kitchenettes in Cottages and apartments • Scuba amenities • Non-smoking rooms available • Color cable T.V. • Two room apartments • Free shuttle service to and from boat terminal
Address:	328 Sunny Lane • P.O. Box 1505 • Avalon • CA • 90704
Phone Number:	(310) 510-1505 or (800) 310-1505
Rules:	10-day cancellation policy • No smoking in Las Flores rooms
Rate category:	Moderate to expensive
General Comments:	Emphasizing old-world charm, the La Paloma structure is an arrangement of old brickwork, balconies and vine-covered walkways. They have recently built a new room section to their hotel called Las Flores. These units offer larger accommodations and more amenities. Cleaning and storage facilities are available to their scuba diving clientele.

Old Turner Inn

Built:	1927
Map Location:	24
Motif:	Country charm with a touch of romance
No. of Rooms:	5
Rooms w/Ocean View:	None
Features:	Private baths • Heated rooms • Extensive continental breakfast • Lunch and dinner appetizers • Color cable T.V. • Sitting porches in two units • Wood burning fireplaces
Address:	232 Catalina Ave. • P.O. Box 97 • Avalon • CA • 90704
Phone Number:	(310) 510-2236
Rules:	Non-smoking facility • 7-day cancellation policy
Rate category:	Expensive
General Comments:	The Old Turner Inn is a cozy bed & breakfast establishment catering to a fairly small clientele. Gutted and refurbished in 1987, its homey layout reflects a country inn. There are wood burning fireplaces in four of the five rooms, and hand-stitched linens, touches of wicker, brass, and antique furniture in most units.

Pacific Isle Apartments

Built:	1920s
Map Location:	25
Motif:	Contemporary
No. of Rooms:	6
Rooms w/Ocean View.:	2
Features:	Private baths • Heat • Color cable T.V. • King and queen beds • In room refrigerators • Non-smoking rooms available • Kitchenettes in all rooms • Barbecue • Rooms with viewing balconies • Coin-operated washer and dryer •
Address:	330 Whitley Ave. • P.O. Box 2148 • Avalon • CA • 90704
Phone Number:	(310) 510-2721
Rules:	No refunds on cancellations • Smoking regulations
Rate category:	Moderate to expensive
General Comments:	This six-unit complex offers apartment-style living at rates that, when shared with four or six individuals, are very affordable. The hotel was gutted and refurbished in the early 1980s, and now contains modern amenities. The six units consist of two 2-bedroom units, two 1-bedroom units and two studios.

Inn on Mount Ada

Built:	1921
Map Location:	22
Motif:	Georgian Colonial
No. of Rooms:	6
Rooms w/Ocean View:	6
Features:	Private baths with original 1921 tubs • Sun deck patio room • Full breakfast, lunch and dinner • Free use of golf cart for transportation to and from town • Heated rooms • In room fireplaces • Free shuttle service • Scuba amenities • Harbor view terrace • Fully staffed to handle weddings or parties
Address:	398 Wrigley Rd. • P.O. Box 2560 • Avalon • CA • 90704
Phone Number:	(310) 510-2030
Rules:	No smoking • 10-day cancellation policy
Rate category:	Very expensive
General Comments:	Perched high atop Mt. Ada, this Georgian Colonial-style mansion is the former home of William Wrigley, Jr. Named after his wife, Ada, it is the most elegant place to stay in Catalina. Its rooms epitomize romance and luxury. It has been renovated and remodeled with early 1900 antiques. There is a viewing terrace towering high atop the inn, offering a 360 degree panorama of local Catalina. Full meals are provided in the room rate. Dinner includes house wines, beers and champagne. It is listed in the National Register of Historic Places.

Originally the home of William Wrigley, Jr., Inn on Mt. Ada is perhaps the most exquisite place to stay at Catalina. The mansion is equipped with many amenities, including a beautiful viewing terrace that overlooks Avalon Bay (pictured here).

Pavilion Lodge

Built:	1959
Map Location:	26
Motif:	Contemporary
No. of Rooms:	72
Rooms w/Ocean View:	None
Features:	Private baths • Color cable T.V. • Free continental breakfast • Grassy courtyard • Scuba amenities • Air conditioning and heat • Video/VCR rental • King and queen beds • In room refrigerators • Courtesy beach towels • Free shuttle service
Address:	513 Crescent Ave • P.O. Box 737 • Avalon • CA • 90704
Phone Number:	(310) 510-2500 or (800) 626-5440
Rules:	3-day cancellation policy
Rate category:	Expensive
General Comments:	The Pavilion Lodge has in recent years been completely renovated at a price tag of nearly $2,000,000. Brightly decorated in pastels, the rooms are spacious and very clean. Pavilion Lodge itself is only 14-steps from the beach. For its boarding quality, Pavilion Lodge is the recipient of the AAA Three-Diamond award.

Seacrest Inn

Built:	Early 1900s
Motif:	Romantic Victorian
Map Location:	27
No. of Rooms:	7
Rooms w/Ocean View:	None
Features:	Private baths • King and queen size beds • In room refrigerators • Fireplaces in some rooms • Honeymoon amenities • Air conditioning and heat • All nonsmoking rooms • Color cable T.V. with VCR • Whirlpool or fun tub baths • Free continental breakfast
Address:	201 Clarissa Ave. • P.O. Box 128 • Avalon • CA • 90704
Phone Number:	(310) 510-0800
Rules:	Smoking regulations •7-day cancellation policy
Rate category:	Moderate to expensive
General Comments:	Catering to honeymooners and couples in love, Seacrest Inn is the epitome of a romantic bed and breakfast getaway. All rooms have been completely gutted and outfitted with modern elegance; they are decorated in a turn-of-the-century, frilly, romantic country theme, and each bath tub is equipped with a rubber duck, an amenity for their spirited clientele.

Seaport Village Inn

Built:	1983
Map Locatlon:	28
Motif:	Contemporary
No. of Rooms:	44
Rooms w/Ocean View:	6
Features:	Private Baths • Color cable T.V. • Wet bars in suites • Complete kitchen in suites • Scuba amenities • Barbecues • Spa • Sun deck • Air conditioning in some rooms • Coin operated washer & dryer
Address:	119 Maiden Lane • P.O. Box 2411 • Avalon • CA • 90704
Phone Number:	(310) 510-0344
Rules:	7-day cancellation policy
Rate category:	Moderate to expensive
General Comments:	The rooms at Seaport Village are bright and very clean. Each unit has access to a common patio, where you can relax in the spa or use the barbecue. All units are self serviced (no maids). The inn caters heavily to scuba divers, providing gear rinse and storage facilities, and free shuttle service.

Snug Harbor Inn

Built:	Refurbished in 1997
Map Location:	29
Motif:	Nantucket
No. of Rooms:	6
Rooms w/Ocean View:	6
Features:	Private baths • Heated rooms • Free continental breakfast • Non-smoking rooms • Fireplace • Jacuzzi tub • King size beds • T.V. and VCR • CD player • Two phones • In-room safe • Air conditioning
Address:	108 Sumner Ave. • P.O. Box 2470 • Avalon • CA • 90704
Phone Number:	(310) 510-8400
Rules:	No smoking in hotel • 5-day cancellation policy
Rate category:	Expensive
General Comments:	Snug Harbor Inn is a refurbished circa 1900 building. Proprieties have set a cozy atmosphere by creating rooms with exotic bed linens, and feather beds. The rooms have security measures which include in-room safes so guests can store valuable items. Although the hotel caters to upper class living, guests seek its atmosphere due to the elegance offered by the operation.

Zane Grey Hotel

Built:	1926
Map Location:	30
Motif:	Southwestern
No. of Rooms:	18
Rooms w/Ocean View:	7
Features:	Private baths • Heated rooms • Community microwave & refrigerator • Swimming pool • Free shuttle service • Free continental breakfast • Non-smoking rooms • Viewing deck • Lobby fireplace
Address:	199 Chimes Tower Rd. • P.O. Box 216 • Avalon • CA • 90704
Phone Number:	(310) 510-0966 or (800) 3-PUEBLO
Rules:	No smoking in hotel • 5-day cancellation policy
Rate category:	Moderate
General Comments:	Zane Grey Pueblo is the former home of novelist Zane Grey, who lived here from 1926 until his death in 1939. He designed the hotel as a Hopi Indian-style pueblo, where he would spend his days writing novels. Today, the hotel remains much like it was decades ago. Each room is aptly named after a Zane Grey novel. Upstairs, a viewing deck allows hotel guests to experience the spectacular sweeping vista of Avalon Bay. Outside in the garden terrace is a sparkling swimming pool for guest use, one of a few on the island.

Hotels in Two Harbors

Banning House

Built:	1910
Map Location:	N/A
Motif:	Early 19th century rustic
No. of Rooms:	11
Rooms w/Ocean View.:	10
Features:	Private baths • In-house dining during winter • Free shuttle service • Large rooms • Beautiful sunroom • Large common living room • Scuba gear storage and rinsing facilities in town
Address:	Box 5044-BHL • Two Harbors • Catalina Isl. • CA • 90704
Phone Number:	(310) 510-2800
Rules:	14-day cancellation policy
Rate category:	Moderate to expensive
General Comments:	Located in Two Harbors, the Banning House was built as a summer home for the Banning brothers, who for a time during the early 1900's, owned Santa Catalina Island. Originally constructed high atop a hill in 1910, the house was converted into a bed and breakfast resort lodge in 1987, all while retaining its 1900 lore.
	The most luxurious room at the Banning House is perhaps the Crow's Nest, located above the main house. This room has a spectacular panoramic view of Isthmus Cove and is very popular among romantics. Cliff House East and Cliff House West offer beautiful, sweeping views of Catalina Harbor; guests can also watch the sun set from the comfort of their rooms. For tranquility, there are no phones or T.V.'s in any rooms.

The Banning House, once owned by the Banning brothers at the turn of the century, has since been converted into a beautiful lodge. The rooms have kept their antiquated lore, and most are poised to view Cat Harbor or Isthmus Cove.

Hotel Locator Map

Key Points Review

◻ Make all reservations well in advance (4 - 8 weeks) during peak season (April to October). One week is sufficient during the rest of the year.

◻ Have a booking confirmation sent to you by mail

◻ Verify bookings several days before your arrival

◻ If an ocean view is desired, specifically request it.

◻ A few hotels are share-bath, privacy is minimal as a result.

◻ Ask about whether your hotel provides complimentary baggage service

◻ Avalon Baggage Service will provide transportation for those with large amounts of baggage. Rates vary with baggage loads. Call Avalon Baggage Service at (310) 510-2888.

◻ Shop around for weekend and midweek specials

◻ Most hotels will work with you to arrange tour packages

◻ Minimum two night stay required at many hotels, particularly on weekends in season

◻ Be aware of the hotel's cancellation policy

◻ Be sure that hotels are "truly" scuba friendly

Hotel Quick Reference

Map Location	Scuba Friendly	Hotel	Phone	Price Category	Scuba Storage	Freshwater Rinse	# of Rooms	Rooms w/Ocean View	Page
1	Yes	Atwater Hotel	(800) 322-3434	Bu-Mod	Room	No	100	25	52
N/A	Yes	Banning House	(310) 510-2800	Mod-Exp	Yes	Yes	11	10	70
2	Yes	Bayview	(310) 510-7070	Budget	Yes	Yes	20	4	52
3	No	Buena Vista	(310) 510-0340	Bu-Mod	No	No	10	4	53
4	Yes	Casa Mariquita	(800) 545-1192	Mod-V Exp	Room	Yes	22	7	53
5	Yes	Catalina Beach House	(800) 97-HOTEL	Moderate	Yes	Yes	23	2	54
6	Yes	Catalina Canyon	(800) 253-9361	Moderate	Yes	Yes	80	0	55
7	Yes	Catalina C./Hermosa H.	(888) 684-1313	Mod-Exp	Yes	No	56	0	54
8	No	Catalina Island Inn	(310) 510-1623	Mod-Exp	No	No	36	10	56
9	No	Catalina Lodge	(800) 974-1070	Moderate	Yes	Yes	15	0	57
10	Yes	Catherine	(310) 510-0170	Moderate	Yes	Yes	15	3	57
11	Yes	Cloud "7"	(800) 422-6836	Moderate	Yes	Yes	17	5	58
12	Yes	Edgewater	(800) 89-HOTEL	Exp-V Exp	Yes	Yes	8	2	58
13	Yes	El Terado Terrace	(800) 540-0139	Bu-Exp	Room	Yes	18	6	59
14	No	Glenmore Plaza	(800) 4-CATALINA	Expensive	No	No	50	8	60
15	Yes	Hotel Catalina	(310) 510-0027	Moderate	Yes	Yes	32	10	59
16	Yes	Hotel Mc Rae	(800) 698-2266	Mod-Exp	Yes	Yes	24	4	61
17	No	Hotel Metropole	(800) 541-8528	Mod-Exp	No	No	47	6	62
18	No	Hotel St. Lauren	(310) 510-2299	Mod-Exp	No	No	42	3	61
19	No	Hotel Villa Portofino	(800) 34-OCEAN	Mod-Exp	No	No	34	5	63
20	Yes	Hotel Vincentes	(310) 510-1115	Mod-V Exp	Yes	Yes	12	2	63
21	No	Hotel Vista Del Mar	(310) 510-1452	Mod-V Exp	No	No	15	2	64
22	Yes	Inn on Mount Ada	(310) 510-2030	Very Exp	Yes	Yes	6	6	66
23	Yes	La Paloma /Las Flores	(800) 310-1505	Mod-Exp	Yes	Yes	20	5	64
24	No	Old Turner Inn	(310) 510-2236	Expensive	No	No	5	0	65
25	No	Pacific Isle Apts.	(310) 510-2721	Mod-Exp	No	No	6	2	65
26	Yes	Pavilion Lodge	(800) 626-5440	Expensive	Yes	No	72	0	67
27	No	Seacrest Inn	(310) 510-0800	Mod-Exp	No	No	7	0	67
28	Yes	Seaport Village Inn	(310) 510-0344	Mod-Exp	Yes	Yes	44	6	68
29	No	Snug Harbor Inn	(310) 510-8400	Very Exp	No	No	6	6	68
30	No	Zane Grey	(310) 510-0966	Moderate	No	No	18	7	69

Hotel pricing categories:

Budget: $35 to $60 per night   **Moderate:** $61 to $125 per night
Expensive: $126 to $200 per night   **Very Expensive:** $201 to $550 per night

RESTAURANTS

Avalon has perhaps the greatest diversity of restaurants in one square mile than anywhere else in the world. According to many island locals, guests from other continents have praised not only Catalina's culinary diversity, but its food quality as well. Depending on ones mood, diners may choose to eat at one of the superb ocean front establishments or a secluded restaurant tucked away along one of Avalon's side-streets.

Island guests have a large selection of food themes to consider including steak, seafood, Mexican, Chinese, and Italian. If sit-down meals do not fit your schedule or preference, there are a variety of takeout options. Dotted throughout the city are many interesting fast-food restaurants specializing in anything from hot dogs, hamburgers and sandwiches to tacos, fish & chips, ice cream and pastries.

Though a few unique Avalon eateries have come and gone, most have withstood the economic pressures associated with poor off-season crowds. Survival means that many of Catalina's restaurants close their doors during weekdays in the off-season, but are open on weekends.

About the Restaurant Descriptions

The following descriptions are intended to provide general insight into each Avalon restaurant, allowing the reader to narrow down their culinary option to either their diet preference, budget, or atmosphere. For clarity, below is a brief narrative about each restaurant category.

Map Location: Depicts the restaurant location via a number placed on the map that concludes this chapter.

Main Theme: This category lists the restaurant's basic dining theme. If a classification states "Italian," then that is the fundamental cuisine. However, other non-traditional dishes, such as steaks, may be served. Rick's Cafe, for example, is a classic Italian establishment, but their menu also includes a selection of prime rib, steak, chicken and seafood.

Phone: To use for reservations or general contact information.

Address: The actual street location is provided for ease of finding the restaurant when cruising the streets.

Dining type: If the restaurant is a fast food establishment, offers take-out options, or is a traditional sit down-type eatery, it is noted under this category.

Meals Served: Some restaurants serve breakfast, lunch and dinner while others concentrate on specific meal types. This category states what meal types (breakfast, lunch or dinner) are served at that restaurant.

Payment: The payment category is intended to provide payment options for each restaurant. Though all Catalina restaurants welcome cash, many do not honor credit cards, and most will not accept personal checks. There have been instances, for example, where customers will dine in a restaurant intending to pay with a Visa, unaware that the establishment does not accept credit cards. This category is intended to help customers avoid this type of confusion. As a whole, the lion's share of restaurants honor Visa and MasterCard, but many do not accept American Express. Be sure to verify what credit cards are welcome before dining.

Comments: Many restaurants offer specialty menu items, unique atmospheres, and amusing entertainment. The comments heading partly details these attributes.

Tipping: Although not part of each restaurant description, I offer the following suggestions on tipping. Some dine-in establishments automatically compute a 15 percent gratuity into the bill for groups of six or more. Be sure to read your check carefully so you don't add an additional 15 percent...*bon appétit!!*

Antonios Original

Map Location:	1
Main Theme:	Italian
Phone:	(310) 510-0060
Address:	114 Sumner
Dining type:	Take out & Dine In
Meals:	Lunch & Dinner
Payment:	Cash & Credit
Comments:	Throw your peanut shells on the floor! • Juke box music of the 50's • House Specialty: Day Old Spaghetti • Pizza
Avg. Cost:	L=$5-$10 D=$7-$14

Antonios Pizzeria & Catalina Cabaret

Map Location:	2
Main Theme:	Italian
Phone:	(310) 510-0008
Address:	230 Crescent Ave
Dining type:	Take out & Dine in
Meals:	Breakfast, Lunch & Dinner
Payment:	Cash & Credit
Comments:	Hearty breakfasts • Dixieland Jazz • Color-a-dollar • Specialties..Catalina Calzone, Pizza & Omelettes • Ocean Front
Avg. Cost:	B=$4-$7 L=$5-$10 D=$6-$15

Avalon Bake Shoppe

Map Location:	3
Main Theme:	Pastries
Phone:	(310) 510-0361
Address:	122 Catalina Ave. Near base of green pier
Dining type:	Fast food & Take out
Meals:	Breakfast
Payment:	Cash only
Comments:	Donuts, pastries & bread • Coffee • Everything baked fresh daily • Special order cakes
Avg. Cost:	B=$.30-$2

Armstrong's Seafood

Map Location:	4
Main Theme:	Seafood
Phone:	(310) 510-0113
Address:	306 Crescent
Dining type:	Dine in
Meals:	Lunch & Dinner
Payment:	Cash & Credit
Comments:	Fresh Seafood Market & Restaurant • Ocean Front • Specialty: Swordfish & Catalina Sand Dabs.
Avg. Cost:	L=$7-$11 D=$13-$25

Avalon Seafood

Map Location:	5
Main Theme:	Seafood
Phone:	(310) 510-0197
Address:	Pleasure Pier
Dining type:	Take out and Fast food
Meals:	Lunch & Dinner
Payment:	Cash only
Comments:	Fish & Chips • Waterfront • Shrimp Cocktails
Avg. Cost:	L=$5-$7 D=$5-$7

Blue Parrot

Map Location:	6
Main Theme:	Seafood • Steak • Cajun
Phone:	(310) 510-2465
Address:	Corner of Front & Metropole
Dining type:	Dine in
Meals:	Lunch & Dinner
Payment:	Cash and Credit
Comments:	Great view from every table • Jazz Entertainment • Specialties: Louisiana Chicken & Salmon
Avg. Cost:	L=$6-$8 D=$9-$15

Buffalo Nickel

Map Location:	7
Main Theme:	Mexican
Phone:	(310) 510-1323
Address:	Near Pebbly Beach Helipad • Shuttle Service Available
Dining type:	Take out • Dine in • Fast food
Meals:	Lunch & Dinner
Payment:	Cash and credit
Comments:	Specialties: Pizza, Mexican dishes • Free shuttle to and from Avalon
Avg. Cost:	L=$6-$13 D=$6-$13

Busy Bee

Map Location:	8
Main Theme:	Seafood • Burgers • Steak
Phone:	(310) 510-1983
Address:	304 Crescent Street
Dining type:	Dine in
Meals:	Breakfast, Lunch & Dinner
Payment:	Cash & Credit
Comments:	Oceanfront location • Relaxing atmosphere • Thick Burgers • Homemade soups
Avg. Cost:	B=$7-$8 L=$8-$10 D=$12-$14

Café Prego

Map Location:	9
Main Theme:	Italian • Seafood
Phone:	(310) 510-1218
Address:	603 Crescent Ave.
Dining type:	Dine in
Meals:	Lunch & Dinner
Payment:	Cash & Credit
Comments:	Award winning restaurant • Specialty: Meatless minestrone • Garlic bread • Romantic atmosphere
Avg. Cost:	L=$9-$15 D=$9-$35

Catalina Canyon Grill

Map Location:	11
Main Theme:	Seafood • Steak
Phone:	(310) 510-0327
Address:	883 Los Lomos Rd.
Dining type:	Dine in
Meals:	Breakfast, lunch and dinner
Payment:	Cash & Credit
Comments:	Inland Avalon location • House specialties: Clambake, Canyon Club, Rack of ribs • Outdoor patio service
Avg. Cost:	B=$4-$9 L=$6-$12 D=$7-$35

Channel Hopper

Map Location:	12
Main Theme:	Sandwiches & Chips
Phone:	(310) 510-1971
Address:	Located where the cross channel boats leave
Dining type:	Fast food take out
Meals:	Lunch
Payment:	Cash only
Comments:	Makes hearty sandwiches to go • Call ahead to pre-order before boat leaves • Soups • Souvenirs
Avg. Cost:	L=$3-$5

Channel House

Map Location:	13
Main Theme:	Seafood • Steaks • Pasta
Phone:	(310) 510-1617
Address:	205 Crescent Ave
Dining type:	Dine in
Meals:	Lunch & Dinner
Payment:	Cash & Credit
Comments:	Oceanfront location • Large selection of Cognacs • Weddings • Specialties: Scampi Provencale & Grand Marnier souffle
Avg. Cost:	L=$6-$10 D=$14-$25

Coney Island West

Map Location:	14
Main Theme:	Hot dogs • Burgers • Ice cream
Phone:	(310) 510 0763
Address:	Corner of Crescent & Metropole
Dining type:	Fast food
Meals:	Lunch & dinner
Payment:	Cash only
Comments:	Hot dogs • Burgers • Chile • Ice Cream
Avg. Cost:	L=$2-$4 D=$2-$4

Coyote Joe's

Map Location:	15
Main Theme:	Mexican • American
Phone:	(310) 510-1176
Address:	113 Catalina Ave.
Dining type:	Fast food, take out & dine in
Meals:	Lunch & dinner
Payment:	Cash & Credit
Comments:	Tasty tacos • Sidestreet location • Café-type service
Avg. Cost:	L=$3-$5 D=$4-$7

Descanso Beach Club

Map Location:	16
Main Theme:	Seafood • Steaks • Sandwiches
Phone:	(310) 510-7408
Address:	First civilization past Casino
Dining type:	Dine in
Meals:	Lunch & dinner
Payment:	Cash & credit (Amex Accepted)
Comments:	Cocktail bar • Tropical atmosphere • Private parties encouraged • Cocktails allowed on beach • Beach fee of $1.50
Avg. Cost:	L=$3-$9 D-$7-$17

El Galleon

Map Location:	17
Main Theme:	Steaks & Seafood
Phone:	(310) 510-1188
Address:	411 Crescent Ave. Near green pier
Dining type:	Dine in
Meals:	Lunch & dinner
Payment:	Cash & Credit
Comments:	Street front location • Entertainment • Excellent atmosphere • Specialty: Swordfish Steak
Avg. Cost:	L=$6-$13 D=$8-$30

Erics

Map Location:	18
Main Theme:	Burgers • Chile • Omelets
Phone:	(310) 510-0894
Address:	On the green Pleasure Pier
Dining type:	Fast food & take out
Meals:	Breakfast & lunch
Payment:	Cash only
Comments:	Good atmosphere • Must keep alcohol behind white line • Specialty: Buffalo burgers
Avg. Cost:	B=$3-$5 L=$4-$6

Joe's Place

Map Location:	19
Main Theme:	Omelets • Pancakes • Hamburgers
Phone:	(310) 510-0491
Address:	At base of Green Pleasure Pier
Dining type:	Fast food, take out or dine in
Meals:	Breakfast, lunch & dinner
Payment:	Cash & Credit
Comments:	Coffee shop • Good omelets • Tasty Pancakes • Opens at 6:00 a.m. • Gets crowded fast
Avg. Cost:	B=$3-$5 L=$4-$7 D=$4-$8

Kentucky Fried Chicken Taco Bell

Map Location:	20
Main Theme:	Chicken & Tacos
Phone:	(310) 510-2147
Address:	107 Metropole
Dining type:	Fast food
Meals:	Lunch & dinner
Payment:	Cash only
Comments:	Makes chicken, Tacos & Burritos
Avg. Cost:	L=$3-$6 D=$3-$6

Lady Catherine's

Map Location:	21
Main Theme:	Seafood • Hamburgers
Phone:	(310) 510-0170
Address:	708 Crescent (In the Catherine Hotel)
Dining type:	Dine in
Meals:	Lunch & dinner
Payment:	Cash & credit
Comments:	Quaint atmosphere • Pricey • Champagne brunch • Specialty: Swordfish
Avg. Cost:	L=$9-$11 D=$11-$17

The Landing Bar & Grill

Map Location:	22
Main Theme:	Sandwiches • Seafood • Chicken
Phone:	(310) 510-1474
Address:	101 Marilla Ave (Inside the Encanto arch)
Dining type:	Take out & dine in
Meals:	Lunch & dinner
Payment:	Cash & credit (Amex accepted)
Comments:	Gourmet seafood meals upstairs to pizza and sandwiches downstairs • Patio seating • 14 micro brewery beers
Avg. Cost:	L=$5-$10 D=$5-$20

Lori's Good Stuff

Map Location:	23
Main Theme:	Sandwiches • Health food • Vegetarian
Phone:	(310) 510-2489
Address:	510 Crescent
Dining type:	Fast food & take out
Meals:	Lunch
Payment:	Cash only
Comments:	Fruit shakes • Hearty sandwiches • Salads
Avg. Cost:	L=$3-$5

Luau Larry's

Map Location:	24
Main Theme:	Seafood • Sandwiches • Chicken
Phone:	(310) 510-1919
Address:	509 Crescent
Dining type:	Dine in
Meals:	Breakfast, lunch & dinner
Payment:	Cash & Credit
Comments:	Polynesian atmosphere • Wild! • Excellent food • Great chicken dishes • Try their Wednesday cheese burger
Avg. Cost:	B=$5.95 L=$5-$10 D=$5-$10

Mi Casita

Map Location:	25
Main Theme:	Mexican
Phone:	(310) 510-1772
Address:	111 Clarissa
Dining type:	Dine in
Meals:	Lunch & dinner
Payment:	Cash & Credit
Comments:	Food homemade daily • Sidestreet location • Specialties: Steak adobado, carnitas, and carne asada
Avg. Cost:	L=$5-$6 D=$9-$12

Mr. Ning's Chinese Garden

Map Location:	26
Main Theme:	Chinese • Vegetarian
Phone:	(310) 510-1161
Address:	127 Sumner St.
Dining type:	Fast food, take out or dine in
Meals:	Lunch & dinner
Payment:	Cash & Credit
Comments:	An island favorite • Superb Chinese dishes • Excellent hot & sour soup! • $3 minimum per person
Avg. Cost:	L=$5-$8 D=$8-$18

Pancake Cottage

Map Location:	27
Main Theme:	Pancakes • Omelets • Burritos
Phone:	(310) 510-0726
Address:	118 Catalina Ave.
Dining type:	Dine in
Meals:	Breakfast & lunch
Payment:	Cash & Credit
Comments:	Excellent waffles • Gets crowded in a.m. • Many types of pancakes: chocolate, banana, pecan. Filling!
Avg. Cost:	B=$4-$8 L=$4-$8

Pete's Plaza Café

Map Location:	28
Main Theme:	Omelets • Sandwiches
Phone:	(310) 510-0523
Address:	128D Sumner Ave. (Located in tour bus plaza)
Dining type:	Fast food & take out
Meals:	Breakfast & lunch
Payment:	Cash only
Comments:	Outdoor patio seating • Quiet • Serves a mean omelet • Chili fries
Avg. Cost:	B=$4-$7 L=$3-$5

Rick's Cafe

Map Location:	29
Main Theme:	Italian
Phone:	(310) 510-0333
Address:	417 Crescent
Dining type:	Dine in
Meals:	Lunch & dinner
Payment:	Cash & Credit
Comments:	Ocean view • Romantic atmosphere • Catering for up to 100 • Specialty: Swordfish stuffed with shrimp & crab
Avg. Cost:	B=$5-$11 L=$6-$14 D=$9-$25

Ristorante Villa Portofino

Map Location:	30
Main Theme:	Italian
Phone:	(310) 510-0508
Address:	101 Crescent Ave.
Dining type:	Dine in
Meals:	Dinner
Payment:	Cash & credit
Comments:	Award winning restaurant • Pleasant atmosphere • Specialties: Braciole di Vittello and Ravioli di Murano
Avg. Cost:	D=$6-$21

Salley's Waffle Shop

Map Location:	31
Main Theme:	Omelets • Waffles • Burgers
Phone:	(310) 510-0355
Address:	505 Crescent
Dining type:	Dine in
Meals:	Breakfast & lunch
Payment:	Cash & credit
Comments:	Scrumptious Waffles: Pecan, strawberry, and More! • Tasty veggie-burgers, too • Oceanfront location • Fast service
Avg. Cost:	B=$4-$6 L=$5-$6

The Sand Trap

Map Location:	32
Main Theme:	Omelets • Burgers
Phone:	(310) 510-1349
Address:	On Avalon Canyon Rd. towards Botanical Garden
Dining type:	Take out & dine in
Meals:	Breakfast & Lunch
Payment:	Cash only
Comments:	Enjoy a golf atmosphere • ¾ of a mile from town. Specialties: Turkey tacos, Bogie Burgers, and Huevos rancheros
Avg. Cost:	B=$3-$7 L=$3-$7

Casino Dock Cafe

Map Location:	33
Main Theme:	Sandwiches • Salads • Burgers
Phone:	(310) 510-2755
Address:	Near the gas dock at Casino Point
Dining type:	Fast food & take out
Meals:	Breakfast & lunch
Payment:	Cash only
Comments:	Pier location • Hot food • Ideal for divers at Underwater Park
Avg. Cost:	B=$4-$5 L=$4-$8

Doug's Harbor Reef

Map Location:	N/A
Main Theme:	Steaks • Seafood
Phone:	(310) 510-0303
Address:	Two Harbors
Dining type:	Dine in
Meals:	Dinner year round • Breakfast, lunch and dinner from July thru August
Payment:	Cash & Credit
Comments:	Overlooking beach & ocean • Try a "Buffalo Milk" • Swordfish & Prime rib • Catering for groups of 500 and more
Avg. Cost:	D=$13-$20

The Reef Grill

Map Location:	N/A
Main Theme:	Sandwiches • Snacks
Phone:	(310) 510-0303
Address:	Two Harbors
Dining type:	Fast food & take out
Meals:	Breakfast & lunch
Payment:	Cash only
Comments:	Quick service food depot • Mouth- watering sandwiches • Omelets • Oceanfront location
Avg. Cost:	B=$4-$5 L=$3-$6

Ship Rock Cafe

Map Location:	N/A
Main Theme:	Mexican • Pizza • Deli Sandwiches
Phone:	(310) 510-2755
Address:	Isthmus Cove
Dining type:	Fast food & Take out
Meals:	Lunch & Dinner
Payment:	Cash & Credit
Comments:	Off beach • Dancing • Games • Activities
Avg. Cost:	L=$3-$6 D=$4-$7

Runway Café

Map Location:	N/A
Main Theme:	Sandwiches • Burgers
Phone:	(310) 510-2196
Address:	At Airport In The Sky
Dining type:	Fast food
Meals:	Breakfast & Lunch
Payment:	Cash & Credit
Comments:	At Catalina's airport • Near Nature Center • Specialty: Buffalo burgers • Buffalo Jerky
Avg. Cost:	B=$2-$5 L=$3-$6

Twilight Dining Tour

Map Location:	N/A
Main Theme:	Seafood • Steak • Prime rib
Phone:	(310) 510-2500
Address:	Reservations: Visitor's Information Center
Dining type:	Dine in
Meals:	Dinner cruise
Payment:	Cash & credit
Comments:	Depart Avalon and cruise along 14 miles of Catalina's scenic coastline. Disembark at Two Harbors for a sumptuous buffet • Music & dancing • 5½ hours long
Avg. Cost:	D=$35

Restaurant Locator Map

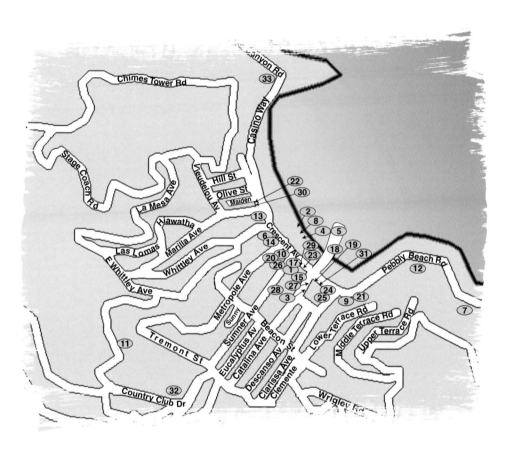

HISTORICAL POINTS OF INTEREST

Tuna Club

The 1898 formation of the Tuna Club would forever change the fishing ethics at Catalina. It all started when famous writer Charles Frederick Holder, also a master angler and devout sportsman, visited Catalina for the first time in 1887. What he saw upon his arrival was the sad reality of hand-lining. This fishing practice utilized strong, unbreakable lines, by which hooked fish had little chance of escaping. Local anglers lined the beaches and, one after another, callously hoisted ashore enormous yellowtail and white seabass.

Holder departed the island in disgust, but later returned with some lightweight fishing hardware that consisted of a nine-foot divine fishing rod and some makeshift fly tackle. This was the first ever documented fishing tackle at Catalina Island. Holder, using his angling prowess, finally cast line for the first time in Catalina waters. Strike after strike, Holder

Though many fisherman have spent years trying to catch a properly sized fish to become inaugurated into the Tuna Club, Winston Churchill did it by landing this 188 pound marlin 30 minutes after leaving the dock in Avalon. (Photo Courtesy of SCICo)

Near the turn of the century, the large and plentiful marine life at Catalina attracted fishermen from around the world. This had a significant and positive influence on a growing tourist market. Here, a Mola mola shows just how large fish were during this era. (Photo Courtesy of SCICo)

found the fight to be a real challenge; he landed some yellowtail and lost others. Over the next several years, as word of Catalina's aquatic fruitfulness reached far across the nation to other sporting anglers, fishing with rod and reel became more popular at this island paradise.

In 1898, Holder surprised the world by landing a 183-pound tuna at Catalina on rod and reel. This was the first documented large tuna ever caught on this type of gear. The word of his magnificent catch reached papers across the globe, thus further boosting Catalina as a world-renowned fishing haven. Holder knew that the time to discourage hand-lining at Catalina and establish true fishing ethics was here.

Holder's love for the sport, coupled with his appreciation for natural history and conservation, led him to the idea of forming a fishing club that promoted fair play for the fish that anglers regularly sought. In June of 1898, he persuaded four of his closest fishing colleagues, H.K. Macomber, E.L. Doran, C.R. Scudder and Fitch Dewey, to form a fishing club. After a period of writing strict fishing rules, club initiation guidelines, and forming a board of governors, the Tuna Club came to fruition. Their motto: fair play for game fishes.

The Tuna Club was built after the turn of the century. It is still today used as a meeting place for gentleman anglers.

The Tuna Club was also the first organization that actually recognized an angler for demonstrating skill while using balanced tackle intended to give the fish a fighting chance. Its formation in 1898 was a departure from the slaughter and early ethics of the fishing industry. Club rules strictly prohibit "hand-lining" and the taking of game fish for commercial purposes. Today, gentlemen anglers continue to meet in the same Tuna Club building they erected in November of 1916.

Airport in the Sky

Prior to 1940, the only way to make an aerial visit to Catalina was by amphibian craft. In 1934, the Wrigley's took the first steps to build an airport. Engineers set up weather stations at potential landing sites around the island and monitored them for five years. The basic goal was to determine the best possible landing approach as it related to prevailing winds. After the site was chosen in 1940, work crews graded a mountainous, yet climatically optimal, area and formed a runway. The runway operated without surfacing until 1946, when workers paved it, and built a terminal building.

The airport, however, was not without political involvement. During its construction in the early 1940s, world tensions escalated, leading to U.S. involvement in WWII. War activities led the Santa Catalina Island Company (SCICo) to prevent possible enemy landings by blockading the runway. SCICo directors eventually rented the airport to the Army for $1 per year. When U.S. war interests dissolved, the airport reopened. However, the public did not have access to it until 1959.

Called the "Airport in the Sky" because of its 1,602-foot elevation, the facility utilizes a 3,200 foot runway. Though pilots ably landed 26-passenger DC-3's here decades ago, today's visiting aviators land planes that are comparatively much smaller. The landing strip has a visual enigma that many call a "bump" or false horizon. Pilots occasionally abort landings because it provides an illusion that the runway is shorter than it really is.

After the airport's construction in 1946, Santa Catalina Island Company contractors constructed a paved commuter road between the airport and Avalon, providing pilots and their passengers easy access to civilization. This led to a considerable increase in aerial visitors. On average, annual landings approach 20,000.

Casino

When William Wrigley Jr. purchased Catalina in 1919, his goal was to provide entertainment for island visitors. Over the first few years of his ownership, Wrigley recognized the need for a special attraction that would entertain and overwhelm island visitors. The result was construction of the spectacular Casino building. Following is a brief synopsis of the Casino's emergence.

When Catalina's visitor trade began to outgrow the first casino building, Sugar Loaf (which had a capacity for 250 people), it was a sure sign times were changing and something fresh and new was needed. In February of 1928, work crews dismantled Sugar Loaf Casino. They moved and reassembled its octagonal steel frame at Catalina's bird park, where it was to serve as the framework for the world's largest bird cage.

Ideally, Wrigley wanted to replace Sugar Loaf Casino with a larger building of Moorish style, with a ballroom stacked atop a theater. To do this, he summoned architects Walter Webber and Sumner A. Spaulding. According to architect Walter Webber: "This point of land being triangular dictated a circular building as the most logical solution. The diameter of the building is the maximum that would fit upon this site" (Moore, 1979).

All the steel pieces that make up the framework of the Casino were cut on the mainland then delivered to Catalina and pieced together like a complex jigsaw puzzle. Amazingly, all the pieces fit nicely together during the assembly. (Photo Courtesy of SCICo)

Construction of the Casino began in March of 1928. Gas shovels helped dig as deep as 40 feet into the bedrock, at which time workers sank supporting shafts. This was followed by laying out floors using 10-inch timber forms, then pouring nearly eight tons of concrete into each shaft.

The next major step was building the steel frame. David M. Renton, Wrigley's master builder on Catalina, sums up the assembly of the steel pieces in a letter he wrote to a fellow associate: "One of the items which impressed me forcibly was the fact that out of a great many pieces of steel going into this building, they all dovetailed in nicely; no errors or delays, and everything was perfected in the shop before being delivered on the job." In total, the Casino's framework consists of 28,222 steel shapes and plates. (Moore, 1979)

Catalina's Casino was officially opened on May 29, 1929. The grand opening brought forth a flurry of activities, including a flag raising, a parade, music, and tours of the building, to name a few.

Following the framework, workers poured the concrete walls and performed a jigsaw of brickwork. This required nearly 25,000 yards of concrete and 15,000 bricks. Artists then put the final touches on the new building in a matter of a few months. Some noted artistic accents include John Beckman's murals he painted on the walls of the theater and outside walls near the main entrance. Artists also used 60,000 4-inch squares of silver leaf and 500 square feet of 22-karat gold leaf to accentuate various areas of the building.

The Casino officially opened on May 29, 1929. Its two principal features are the theater and ballroom.

1. Theater: Engineers designed the theater with true acoustic expertise, layering the floor with cork so sound carried better. The acoustics are so good that patrons can hear a normal conversation from the other side of the 138-foot diameter room. Seating capacity is 1,184. Within the confines of the room are spectacular murals painted by artist John Beckman and his staff of gifted

Many of the murals painted by artist John Beckman depict his unique vision of Catalina's marine world.

craftsmen. The murals are further emphasized with brilliantly colored lights, setting a mood of wonder and awe for theater guests.

The acoustics in the Casino theater are so good that it's difficult to tell from which direction sound is coming.

An impressive pipe organ sits near the big screen, built by the Page Company in Lima, Ohio after the turn of the century. The organ is set up with sixteen ranks of pipe (73-85 pipes per rank) which are fitted into ceiling lofts and covered with grill work. Inside the organ are 12,969 individual wire segments, the equivalent of 250 miles of wire. During selected events, a professional organist plays music on this masterpiece of workmanship.

2. Ballroom: The ballroom is cantilevered; there are no interrupted supporting pillars throughout its 180 foot expanse. This design makes it the largest ballroom of its type in existence.

The stylish dance floor is composed of maple strips, white oak and rosewood on top of layers of felt and acoustical paper. These two elements are, in turn, on top of a subfloor of polished pine floating on cork. The apex of the ballroom contains a chandelier, which hides the ventilation system (Moore, 1979). Built into the chandelier are a variety of adjustable colored lights to set specific moods.

The Casino Ballroom hosts numerous functions each year, including parties, weddings and dances. This photo depicts a large crowd dancing to a popular big band of the era. (Photo Courtesy of SCICo)

After becoming a symbol of nationwide entertainment, the Casino attracted many Big Band notables such as Benny Goodman and Jimmy Dorsey, who are among the long list of entertainers that played here. On May 8, 1940, Kay Kyser drew the largest crowd ever in the Casino ballroom—6,200—a far cry from Sugar Loaf Casino's guest capacity of 250. Today, crowds are limited to 1,200 to 1,800, depending on the activity.

Holly Hill House

The Holly Hill House is one of the oldest houses in Avalon. Peter Gano began constructing it in 1888 after he purchased the property from George Shatto for $500. The piece of land on which Gano intended to build his home was high atop a sloping hillside. The question of how to shuttle building materials from the bay uphill to the lot was answered when Gano devised a cable car pulley system that required the use of his horse, Mercury, previously of circus fame. Mercury was trained to walk downhill and to respond to Gano's "whistle" instructions. When Gano wanted to bring up a load of materials, he would whistle and Mercury would walk downhill, pulling the cable car uphill to the house.

After the house was finished in 1890, Gano dubbed it "Look Out Cot." It stands three stories high, encompasses about 3,000 square feet and is one of the first frame homes built in Avalon. The apex of the house contains a prominent cupola, designed to give Gano a view of Avalon and its surrounding waters.

A local island myth tells of Gano's attempt to persuade his fiancé to marry him and move across the sea to Catalina. As the story goes, she had no desire to live an isolated island life and declined Gano's offer. Legend has it that his fiancé announced an ultimatum: choose the house or her. For the next 32 years, Gano lived alone in his island dream home.

In 1921 Gano sold the house to the Giddings family, who subsequently called the abode "Holly Hill House," owing to the abundance of holly plants surrounding the structure. Today, Holly Hill House is the epitome of housing as it was 100 years ago. You can see it perched high atop a hill on the east side of Avalon Harbor.

Built in 1888, Holly Hill House is one of Catalina's oldest structures.

Glass Bottom Boats

The development of glass-bottom boats brought a flourishing trade to modern Catalina. It all began with an Avalon abalone fisherman named Charles Feige. Fishermen had long known that a box with a glass bottom could be used to see animals and objects clearly under the water. But it was Feige who brought further practicality to the idea. In 1896, he built a glass window into one of his rowboat hull's, initially so he could easily spot abalone while on his fishing jaunts. However, there was so much public interest in this rowboat that he began taking passengers on scenic tours of the underwater world. He soon made more profit in glass-bottom boat tours than he did diving for abalone.

Word of his invention spread quickly, and many boatmen became very aggressive about profiting in the new trade. A short time later, an entrepreneur named Captain

Fisherman originally used glass bottom boats to spot abalones along the sea floor.

J.E. Matthewson paid a visit to Avalon while journeying the country. He noted the extreme profit to be made from glass-bottom boats. Shortly after that, Matthewson moved to Avalon and began building his fleet of glass bottom boats powered with oars and strong oarsmen.

Design enhancements made his boats more desirable than those of his competition. Instead of simply building in a glass bottom, which passengers would accidentally step through on occasion, Matthewson built "wells" around the glass, permitting customers to safely lean over the edge to view the aquatic life below. His initial ore-driven boats had a capacity for four passengers, but that soon increased to 25 as the demand accelerated. Woe stricken was the one who used his shoulder and arm muscles to row 25 people!

Motor powered glass-bottom boats made their way into the picture in 1905. In time, better and more expensive boats were introduced: In 1906 Cleopatra, the first paddle wheel propelled glass bottom boat, was introduced at a cost of $15,000. Following that was the launching of Empress in 1917 at a price tag of $25,000. When Wrigley gained ownership of Catalina, he added the Emperor to the fleet, with a cost totaling $65,000. His final contribution to the fleet was the $80,000 Phoenix in 1931, which served the Catalina public until 1994 when it was sold primarily because of its high maintenance costs. Since the Phoenix, a variety of other glass bottom boats have been added to the fleet to help smooth the flow of visiting tourists. The newest under water viewing vessels are the semi submersibles "Starlight," and "Emerald," which are designed so that passengers are actually below the waterline, viewing fish life eye to eye.

Catalina Island Yacht Club

In 1903 big game fishermen at Catalina organized the Sophia Yacht Club and decided to build a clubhouse. After constructing a foundation and sinking some shafts, however, they ran out of money. The piece of land lay dormant until glass-bottom boat magnate J.E. Matthewson used the existing foundation to erect a shop to build his special boats. However, in 1915 the great fire wiped out a third of Avalon, including Matthewson's enterprise.

Catalina Yacht Club.

The charred building lay dormant until the arrival of Art Sanger and his sister Agnes Mondon, who concocted an idea to turn the defunct building into a boat house with a docking facility. They petitioned help from one James Jump, who was responsible for raising revenues to build the club. An agreement was eventually made with the idle Sophia Yacht Club: In exchange for granting use of the vacant property to Jump, Sanger and Mondon, Sophia Yacht Club members could use the club in the wintertime. Catalina Island Yacht Club has since become one of the foremost clubs on the Pacific coast. Its members reside from as far away as Seattle, Washington.

The Wrigley Memorial

This memorial was built in memory of William Wrigley, Jr., who spent twelve years of his life developing Avalon and preserving Catalina's interior.

Work crews began construction of the memorial in October of 1933 and completed it eight months later. The structure is 232 feet wide and 180 feet deep. The memorial's primary attraction is the viewing tower. Though the actual tower is 80 feet high, its base rests atop a 50-foot elevated stairway, providing a total height of 130 feet. Here, guests experience a sweeping panorama of Catalina's rugged hillsides and blue Pacific waters.

Most of the materials used to build the monument were excavated exclusively from Catalina. A goal of the

The Wrigley Memorial.

building's contractors was to show the natural beauty of these excavated materials in as much detail as possible. For example, all of the aggregate used in the concrete was quarried and crushed on Catalina. After the concrete dried, workers removed the timber forms and sandblasted the surface, not only to remove unsightly blemishes left by the forms, but to highlight the colors and textures of the stones used in the aggregate. In addition, architects used blue flagstone rock from Little Harbor extensively on the ramp and on the terraces of the tower to give it a distinctive look.

Arcitecturally speaking, Wrigley employed the use of his own island tile manufacturing plant, which produced the roof tiles and the snappy glazed tiles for the structure's interior. In keeping with a tradition of using all naturally occurring island elements to build the memorial, workers fabricated the glazed tiles from native clay. Finishers applied the final touches and the structure was completed in June of 1934. Wrigley's body was, indeed, enshrined here for a time, but for personal reasons family members eventually relocated Mr. Wrigley to a cemetery plot in Pasadena.

The Botanical Garden

Heeding their desire to maintain a fruitful wilderness at Catalina, Wrigley and his wife, Ada, paid much attention to the interior land, planting trees, shrubs and flowers throughout the island. It was Ada's love of gardening that inspired her husband to bring a horticulturist named Albert Conrad to the island to help plant a garden in Avalon Canyon that would exhibit a variety of exotic and local succulents and cactus.

Though Mrs. Wrigley and Mr. Conrad devised a beautiful garden, more significant improvements were made in 1969. The Wrigley Memorial Garden Foundation decided to improve on the already impressive garden by adding acreage and making the garden more robust. Soon afterwards, the area became known as The Wrigley Memorial Garden. Today, the site is the focal point for observing an enormous variety Catalina's floral species, including plants that are rare and endemic to the island. In total the Monument and Memorial Garden grounds encompass about 32 acres.

The garden is a place of many interests. Numerous wayfarers stroll the memorial grounds because of its peaceful ambiance and the variety of surrounding floral life forms. However, it is a place of education as well. There are interesting horticultural displays that disseminate knowledge to students and visitors. The floral exhibits also allow scientists to study island plants, particularly those endemic to Catalina. Horticulturists are continually enlarging and expanding the Wrigley Botanical Garden with new plant forms. In addition, its educational attributes are endlessly upgraded and made more practical for public and academic use.

The Botanical Garden is home to several floral species that no longer exist on the mainland. Here, springtime flowers accentuate the garden with vibrant hues.

One of the highlights of the Botanical garden is the Cacti sector, where many succulent species exist for the visitor's viewing pleasure.

An aerial shot of Two Harbors shows how narrow the connecting stretch of land really is.

Two Harbors Historical Points of Interest

Near the west end of Catalina is Catalina Harbor (a.k.a. Cat Harbor) and Isthmus Cove, two small inlets on opposing sides of the island joined by less than one-half mile of land. This is called Two Harbors. Two Harbors, for centuries, has been a bounteous source for adventure and history. It served as a small Indian community for the Catalina natives who called themselves Pimugnans. Archeological evidence puts the Pimugnans at Little Harbors as far back as 7,000 years ago; scientists believe that the Indian population averaged 300.

The area suited them ideally because it was spacious and close to the sea. Though fishing was an invaluable asset for Indian survival, they also made <u>ollas</u> (OY- yahs), or stone crock pots, from material they excavated at a soapstone quarry at Empire Landing. The Pimus used the <u>ollas</u> in an extensive trade market with mainland tribes. Archaeologists today continue to find broken <u>olla</u> pieces scattered around the area. Other unique Indian artifacts discovered are bone fishhooks, pipes and soapstone mortars.

Pirates and smugglers also made Two Harbors an infamous Eden of shame. Smugglers loved Cat Harbor because it offered a safe haven from which to rendezvous with other smugglers. Here, illegal trading of goods took place to avoid costly tariffs set by government dignitaries. Perhaps the most famous pirate's vessel to enter the waters of Cat Harbor was the Chinese junk, Ning Po, believed to be the first ship ever to use watertight compartments. Built in 1773, her record includes smuggling, slavery, piracy, and prisoners. Ning Po was also an armed Manchu Rebellion warship, but ended its days as a cafe and museum in Catalina Harbor. Today, she lies embedded in the harbor's mud bottom.

In 1864, the U.S. Army sent 83 men to the Isthmus to take possession of Catalina. Their task was to survey the island as a proposed reservation for militant Indians. Just as a mining boom was taking place on the island, the Army decided Catalina was an ideal location for the troubled Indians, so they ordered the crowd of miners out, and took control of the island. The military built barracks for the troops shortly after the miners left, but they later abandoned the plan to move the Indians to the island. Today, the barracks, built over a century ago, serve as yacht club apartment quarters near the Isthmus harbor office.

The only other significant historical edifice constructed in Two Harbors is the Banning House, built by the Banning brothers in 1910. It has since been used as Coast Guard officer's quarters during WWII and as a private girls camp in the late 1950s. Today it is a 11-room inn called the Banning House Lodge.

As a whole, Two Harbors remains a true wilderness, similar to what it was like when the Catalina Indians lived there. The rustic mood naturally set by this narrow piece of land has made it a favorite backdrop for movie-makers since the early 1900s. Cat Harbor drew most of the attention from Hollywood directors. Its tropical south-seas atmosphere made it a good choice for adventure films of all types. Movies such as Mutiny on the Bounty starring Clark Gable, Treasure Island, and Old Ironsides were filmed here.

The wooden schooners, Palomar and Santa Clara, used in these movies, were left to rot on the sea floor. Occasionally, divers find wreckage and amphoras that they mistake as authentic, but the items are actually movie props. Remains of Jacob's well, used in the filming of the Ten Commandments, lie forgotten on the shores of Two Harbors. At Wells Beach in Cat Harbor, Gregory Peck was filmed reenacting MacArthur's return to the Philippines.

Two Harbors is not only appealing to movie buffs, but also to the educational interests of the public. In 1956, the area around Big Fisherman Cove, east of Isthmus Cove, was the site of a five-acre grant by the Santa Catalina Island Company to the University of Southern California. In 1969, the university established the Marine Science Center, now an institute for marine and coastal studies.

The institute offers several courses for graduate and undergraduate levels, and also provides public tours of the center during summertime. Yet, Two Harbors remains the ultimate attraction. Campers, hikers, scuba divers, kayakers, boaters, archaeologists, biologists, horticulturists and movie-makers thrive off this playground of history, adventure and maritime lore.

CATALINA'S INTERIOR

Throughout time Indians, smugglers, farmers, miners, and even the Army found Catalina to be a special place. Spanning some 47,884 acres, Catalina's interior is a true reminder of what California was like hundreds of years ago. It has survived through years of potential devastation from the introduction of livestock to the ploys of profiteers seeking a quick return.

Though a very small portion of the island is still exploited for breakwater rock, its interior is carefully managed, and open to public visitations. This section will provide a brief look at island management and describe several popular sites within the interior.

Santa Catalina Island Conservancy

Responsibility for maintaining the interior lands lies with the Santa Catalina Island Conservancy. The Wrigley family formed the Conservancy in 1972 for the purpose of protecting and sustaining open-space lands, wild lands and nature preserve areas on Catalina. In 1974 the Santa Catalina Island Company entered into an easement agreement with the County of Los Angeles, granting the county the right to share access to 41,000 acres of Catalina's interior land and some of its coastline for purposes of park, conservation, education and recreation.

On February 15, 1975, the Wrigleys took a giant leap forward by deeding 42,135 acres of Catalina to the Conservancy, which now owns about 86 percent of the island. The Conservancy has a legal directive to preserve Catalina's native plants and animals, biological communities, and geological and geographic formations of academic importance. Included in its responsibilities is the careful management of Catalina's open-space lands. Their goal is to ensure the property is used solely for the enjoyment of its natural beauty and for carefully managed recreation. The Conservancy also works closely with the County of Los Angeles to deliver quality Catalina experiences to the public.

Conservancy projects are many and extremely diverse. Their most publicized is perhaps the Bald Eagle Reintroduction Program. In 1980, the Conservancy, in close association with the Institute for Wildlife Studies and the Los Angeles County Department of Fish and Game, inaugurated a program intended to reintroduce the bald eagle to Catalina. Of 43 released on the island from 1980 to 1995, eight adults and three sub-adults have made permanent homes there. Although the bald eagle was previously a fruitful bird species at Catalina, pesticides and human torment had chiseled away their entire island existence. Today, the bald eagle is a protected species.

Running projects of this nature are costly. Though a legal mandate to preserve Catalina in perpetuity exists, funding of the various projects is entirely up to the Conservancy. They are financed not by our tax dollars, but by private donations, land leases, and various types of other revenue-generating resources.

Points of Interest Within the Interior

Though it might take an almanac to describe "every" interesting area of Catalina Island, this section discusses, in part, frequently visited ones that are typically accessed during general tours. Some locations, however, are only accessible via private tours.

The Conservancy's Nature Center

The Santa Catalina Island Conservancy, in accordance with their educational goals, built the Nature Center, a place where island visitors can see a representation of Catalina's history, biology, archaeology and geology. Located at Catalina's Airport in the Sky, this distinguished attraction features a native plant botanical garden that entertains many of Catalina's endangered and interesting plant species.

The Nature Center offers unique displays that feature Catalina's natural history and wildlife.

The Nature Center also has some of Catalina's native Indian artifacts on display, including jewelry, ollas, and other daily working tools the Indians used. Uniquely poised nearby is a wall display entitled

"Native Animals of Santa Catalina," which discusses the island fox, bald eagle, ornate shrew and two-lined garter snake. Other academic walls discuss archaeology, ecology, geology, history of people, and the marine environment. The Conservancy also constructed a large tile map of Catalina that details island elevations, boundary lines and other interesting features.

El Rancho Escondido

Located in the midst of Catalina's wilderness is a privately owned, 538 acre Arabian horse ranch built in 1932 by William Wrigley's son, Philip. The location he chose to build his ranch was an area near Cottonwood Canyon. The ranch, well concealed beneath cottonwood trees and tricky to locate, was aptly coined El Rancho Escondido (the hidden ranch). After Philip K. Wrigley completed the ranch, he established an Arabian horse breeding program. At one point in the late 1940's, the ranch

El Rancho Escondido is a privately owned Arabian horse ranch built by Philip Wrigley in the early 1930s.

A ranch hand shows a crowd of onlookers how the beautiful Arabian horses perform.

accommodated nearly 75 of these really cool horses. Today those numbers vary between 16 and 20.

In the mid 1980s, the Inland Motor Tour, operated by Santa Catalina Island Company, began making stops at El Rancho Escondido after the Eagle's Nest Lodge stop was terminated. During the visit, tourists can view antiquated stagecoaches that the Wrigleys used to traverse the rugged roads of Catalina in the early 20th century. Additionally, guests may stop by the tack room to see numerous awards, unique bridles and elegant saddles. In my opinion, the bang-for-your-buck attraction during the ranch visit is a narrated show performed by experienced ranch personnel and their gifted Arabian horses. Riders put the pure-breeds through several comical and serious skits that show just how intelligent these horses really are.

After a rest stop at Eagle's Nest Lodge, passengers re-embark their stagecoaches for final passage to Little Harbor Inn. This photo was taken somewhere around the 1890's. (Photo Courtesy of SCICo)

Eagles Nest Lodge

It is thought that one Mr. Daniel A. Baughman built Eagle's Nest Lodge as a hunting lodge in 1896. Historical data suggests that Mr. Baughman probably ran the lodge for the Banning owned Santa Catalina Island Company, living there with his family and running guided hunts with the help of Mexican Joe, an active island outdoorsman.

Hunting parties would depart Avalon via stagecoach or horseback and make their way to Eagle's Nest to take part in guided hunts for eagles, foxes and goats.

A few years later, the lodge closed. However, in 1903 the Santa Catalina Island Company constructed a road connecting Eagle's Nest to Little Harbor on the backside of Catalina. This opened a road system from Avalon to Two Harbors, whose roads meets with Little Harbor. Now that passage from Avalon and other distant

Before paved surfaces were constructed at Catalina, routes to Eagles Nest Lodge and Little Harbor Inn consisted of bumpy, dirt byways. (Photo Courtesy of SCICo)

island locales was possible, stage coaches made frequent trips across the bumpy interior byways. Eagle's Nest Lodge served predominantly as a way station; passengers embarking on the long journey were offered overnight accommodations, and drivers often swapped their tired horses for fresh ones.

In 1910 stage coach service was discontinued. Aside from a few brief occupancies thereafter, Eagle's Nest remained uninhabited until 1935, when Santa Catalina Island Company again used the lodge as hunting headquarters. The lodge offered kitchen and dining facilities, and the area around it was outfitted with tent cabins, or villas, to provide sleeping facilities. Eagle's Nest Lodge was closed in 1942 when the U.S. military took control of Catalina during WWII.

In 1947, the Santa Catalina Island Company began the Inland Motor Tour to provide visitors easy access to Catalina's interior. As part of the tour, Eagle's Nest Lodge was used as a stopover to rest and have

Like Eagles Nest Lodge, farming remnants linger as reminders to modern visitors what the interior was like in full swing nearly 100 years ago.

coffee. Finally, in the mid 1980s, the tour no longer stopped. The building, old and showing the effects of time, has been unused ever since. Luckily, the Catalina Conservancy, who now owns Eagle's Nest Lodge, has plans to refurbish the defunct structure, bringing back a classic memento of Catalina's past, where an eagle's nest was once discovered.

Indian Head Rock

On the backside of Catalina is a rock formation resembling an Indian chief's head. Though one may visit the site anytime of the day and still make out the head, it is best to view it when the sun just begins its downward path to the west. At this time of the day, the sun casts shadows that help accentuate the Indian. One can then clearly discern the chief's mouth, nose, eyes and feathered head dress.

Indian Head Rock just after high noon. Note the shadow the sun casts to help accentuate the eye.

Cottonwood Falls

After adequate rainfall, Catalina's underground springs fill with water. However, because the island's capacity to hold water is exceedingly poor, large quantities seep past the confines of the porous bedrock and form small, serpentine springs that flow down the island's hillsides and into the ocean. One area where water dissemination is prevalent is called Cottonwood Canyon. Here, water exits some 30 feet above the ground, forming Cottonwood Falls. Visiting the site requires a short traverse down a ravine. Be aware that patches of poison oak reside nearby.

Shark Harbor and Little Harbor Overlook

On the ocean side of Catalina are scenic Shark Harbor and Little Harbor. When viewed from high atop the mountainside (overlook), the hillside and ocean scenery is unsurpassed. Little Harbor itself is partially enclosed and protected from prevailing westerly swells, so the water is often flat and glassy.

Cottonwood Falls after a spring rain.

The rare tree poppy clings to much of Catalina's rugged mountainsides and cliffs. During springtime, this unique flower stands out as one of Catalina's most beautiful floral species.

Opposing Little Harbor is Shark Harbor, which is exposed to westerly swells and is consequently a surfing beach. When the sun is shining bright, light rays penetrate deep into the cool water below, turning its hue to a deep metallic blue. White foamy water from nearby pounding surf clashes beautifully with the azure seas.

During springtime brilliantly colored wildflowers outline the shores of the site, providing great natural beauty. If visibility permits, visitors can often see distant Santa Barbara and San Clemente Islands from high atop the overlook.

Cape Canyon Reservoir

Cape Canyon Reservoir is one of several water repositories on Catalina. When the hold is full, it casts a beautiful lake-like setting, hosting exceptionally scenic and peaceful terrain. The site itself is often blessed by the presence of bison, who frequently use it as a watering hole. Under the direction of the Catalina Conservancy, Cape Canyon Reservoir is off limits to anybody other than Conservancy personnel. Thus, to visit it requires a guided "Jeep Eco Tour" offered by the Conservancy.

Cape Canyon Reservoir is a favorite watering hole for Catalina's resident bison.

Bison

Speculation as to how bison were introduced to Catalina still exists today. Some guess that in 1924, film crews delivered 14 bison to Catalina to take part in the filming of a movie. When the crews departed, however, they left the bison behind because rounding them up was too difficult. But historians at Catalina say that no movie ever filmed at Catalina during this era included bison. Thus, the delivery of 14 bison to Catalina is unclear, but the fact that they are there today provides further interest when visiting the interior.

From the initial 14 bison of the early 1920s, the herd increased to 19 by 1934, after which 30 more were shipped to the island from Colorado to supplement the herd. After many annual cycles of reproduction, the herd has grown considerably. Today, bison numbers are carefully controlled at less than 500, since a rampant population would have a devastating effect on Catalina's rare, endangered and biologically important plant and animal communities.

During most inland tours, guests are likely to see some of these island giants at close range. Typically, though, drivers do not allow photographers to leave tour buses, so photo opportunities are not often favorable. However, good photos can be taken during private tours, where guides permit their passengers to shoot pictures outside the vehicle when it is safe.

Tourists are likely to see bison while touring through the interior.

Flora

Within the confines of Catalina's mountains, hills, and valleys are a variety of floral species not found anywhere else in the world, and others that are very rare; many floral species that once thrived along California's coast now flourish solely at Catalina. Consequently, the island is a true symbol of California's past, depicting today what the mainland was like eons ago before humans plowed its soil, paved its surface, and introduced destructive pollutants.

Catalina's herbage is a combination of plant communities: maritime desert scrub, coastal sage scrub and grassland. Maritime desert scrub consists of drought-adapted plants, such as cactuses, that are traditionally found in the dry deserts of Baja, California. One of the more interesting cactus plants is the cholla (CHOY-yah). Not only do the cactus needles protect the plant, but they aid in spreading seeds by attaching to the fur of animals that pass too closely. Far from its parent plant, the needle eventually dislodges and drops to the ground, where it by chance may grow into a new patch of cholla. (Martin, 1988)

Coastal sage scrub communities typically grow near the ocean where the air is moist. These plant communities are recognizable by its dull green or grayish color and pungent sage aroma.

Guests visiting Catalina during springtime experience a dazzling showcase of strange shapes and brilliant colors in the grassland communities. Huge fields of beautiful wildflowers rustle to the beat of prevailing breezes, and cliff-side flowers frame the island in vibrant hues. Some flower species, like the island endemic "Catalina Mariposa Lily" sits perched within prickly-pear cactuses to avoid being eaten by wild animals. Camera buffs be forewarned—photographing this flower at close range could be a painful experience!

Catalina's Physiography Produces Microclimates

Catalina experiences microclimates, which are small, isolated weather patterns that develop throughout the island. Microclimates are most noticed while journeying through Catalina's interior; some areas are foggy and cool while neighboring locales might be sunny and hot. Climatic occurrences of this nature are primarily due to the island's topographical layout of huge canyons, steep cliffs, and extreme variations in elevation. This, coupled with the influences of marine layers on the north facing slopes, shade in the canyons, sun on the south facing slopes, and a potpourri of moist and dry air, produces many unique plant communities and habitats. Interesting endemic and rare life forms could not otherwise exist.

The rare Catalina Mariposa Lily on a mountainside near Two Harbors.

ISLAND TOURS

During the daytime Avalon tour, guides treat passengers to spectacular views of Avalon, like this one shot from the city's back roads.

Stagecoach tours at Catalina began in the 1890's and continued decades thereafter until automobiles were introduced. (Photo Courtesy of SCICo)

The semi-submersible submarine, Starlight, is 60 feet long and holds 36 passengers. It allows onlookers to view beautiful sea life while resting four feet below the waterline.

During the cruise to Seal Rocks, passengers will likely observe sea lions basking lazily in the sun.

Catalina Island has offered tours for years that provide unique insight into island scenery, history and special points of interest. The basic tours range in complexity from 40 minute Avalon tours to private interior excursions.

Operating Status

A few tours are seasonal, operating from April through October, while the majority remain open year round. Though an infrequent occurrence, some tours temporarily close when poor weather arises. When conditions adequately improve, operations resume.

Photography

All tours at Catalina are scenic and memorable; photography is an excellent way to relive your Catalina journeys and remember the island's unique attributes. However, finding yourself short of film is one pitfall photographers frequently experience. Avoid disappointment by packing a few extra rolls. Also, lighting at sites such as the Casino Ballroom is poor for available light photography. A flash unit is often required to get a properly lit picture. Make sure your battery supply is ample, too.

In some areas such as the museum, photography is prohibited; it is always a good idea to ask your guide if there are any particular photo limitations.

Reservations

Most tour operations accept limited reservations, but business by in large is done on a first come, first-served basis. Credit card reservations are accepted for select tours.

Phone numbers for tour operations are listed at the end of this section.

Aerial Tours

Description: Aerial tours offer a fantastic way to view Catalina Island. Depending on the length of the flight, pilots pass through the interior and hug much of the rugged coastline. The ability of the helicopter to move slowly over areas not accessible by the private jeep tours is a significant advantage for sight seers and aerial photographers.

Tour Options	Duration	Presented by
Island Express	30, 20 & 12 minutes	Santa Catalina Island Conservancy

Avalon Tours

Description: Discover enchantment everywhere you turn on a delightful journey along the beach, up the hillsides and through the heart of Avalon. The tour is fun and narrated with interesting Catalina highlights, insights and history.

Tour Options	Duration	Presentod by
Avalon Scenic Tour	50 minutes	Santa Catalina Island's Discovery Tours
Avalon City Tour	50 minutes	Catalina Adventure Tours

Botanical Garden Tours

Description: Combines the Avalon City tour with a stop at the Wrigley Botanical Garden, where guests will see a beautiful garden display developed in part under the guidance of Mrs. Ada Wrigley. Stunning desert plants and unique endemic plants found only on the Channel Islands are among the herbage to view. While at the garden, visit the Wrigley Memorial Monument, where William Wrigley was once buried.

Tour Options	Duration	Presented by
Botanical Garden Tour	1¾ hours	Catalina Adventure Tours
Guided Botanical Garden Tour	2 hours	Santa Catalina Island's Discovery Tours

CasinoTour

Description: Catalina's award-winning landmark has a fascinating history. Discover more about it on this specially guided tour which shows you: The Avalon Theater • A Historical Slide Show • The Casino Ballroom • Art Deco murals • The Casino's Promenade Balcony • The Catalina Island Museum

Tour Options	Duration	Presented by
Casino Tour	40 Minutes	Santa Catilina Island's Discovery Tours

Flying FishTour
(Seasonal tour; operates from April to October)

Description: Board the Blanche W. for an exciting trip to see flying fish. Brilliant 40 million candle power searchlights dramatically spot these aviators of the sea as they glide over the surface of the water.

Tour Options	Duration	Presented by
Flying Fish Boat Trip	55 minutes	Santa Catalina Island's Discovery Tours

Daytime and Nighttime Glass Bottom Boat Tours

Description: Glass bottom boats helped make Catalina famous, and you'll see why during this fun aquatic tour. Peer through the boats' "windows to the undersea world" to watch the colorful fish and unusual marine plants and animals that thrive in the clean water and kelp forest in Lover's Cove Marine Preserve.
Nighttime reveals a whole new scene. Join in the search for ocean night life such as spiny lobsters, moray eels, blacksmith fish, horn sharks, bioluminescent squid and lots more.

Tour Options	Duration	Presented by
Glass Bottom Boat Trip	40 minutes	Canta Catalina Island's DiscoveryTours
Glass Bottom Boat Tour	40 minutes	Catalina Adventure Tours

1¾ Hour Interior Journies

Description: This is an exciting narrated journey along scenic "Skyline Drive" to see spectacular vistas, deep canyons, quiet coves, and blue ocean. Look for bison along the way and visit Catalina's Nature Center exhibits at the Airport-in-the-Sky.

Tour Options	Duration	Presented by
Skyline Drive	2 hours	Santa Catalina Island's Discovery Tours
Inside Adventure Tour	2 hours	Catalina Adventure Tours

4 Hour Interior Journey

Description: Discover the true nature of Catalina on the most detailed interior tour. This 28 mile narrated excursion takes you to the Airport-in-the-Sky and Nature Center—and beyond—to scenic Little Harbor, overlooking Catalina's rugged Pacific side. It's the only way to visit El Rancho Escondido, where you'll be treated to refreshments and an Arabian horse performance.

Tour Options	Duration	Presented by
Inland Motor Tour	3¾ hours	Santa Catalina Island's Discovery Tours

Private Interior Tours

Description: A significant advantage of the private interior tours is that not only does the customer help make the agenda, but the tour vehicles will go almost anywhere that's accessible for public visitation, provided the roads are safe. Points of interest might include Cottonwood Falls, Shark Harbor/Little Harbor Overlook, isolated coves, and rare plant communities. This tour is used frequently by photographers, historians, biologists and tourists.

Tour Options	Duration	Presented by
Jeep Eco Tours	Negotiated	Santa Catalina Island Conservancy
Catalina Safari Tours	Negotiated	Catalina Safari Bus Company
Catalina Transportation Tours	Negotiated	Catalina transportation service

Nature Center Tour

Description: The Santa Catalina Island Conservancy built the Nature Center to provide island guests the opportunity to experience island ecology, geology, biology and history. Guests can tour the center at their leisure or request a guided tour from the Conservancy. Conservancy naturalists may recommend a nature hike in addition to visiting the center itself.

Tour Options	Duration	Presented by
Nature Center Tour	At leisure	Santa catalina Island Conservancy

Sea Lion Tour

Description: Cast off with the Blanche W. to visit Catalina Island's "Showmen of the Sea" at their rugged east end home. The migratory sea lions, more popularly recognized as "trained seals" of circus fame, can be seen swimming and sunning in their natural habitat.

If you are fortunate enough to dive at Seal Rocks, you may have an opportunity to come face to face with many sea lions.

Tour Options	Duration	Presented by
Seal Rocks Cruise	55 minutes	Santa Catalina Island's Discovery Tours

Daytime & Nighttime Semi-Submersible Tours

Description: Join the crew of Starlight, Emerald or Nautilus for an undersea tour of Lover's Cove Marine Preserve. Special underwater windows give you the best view of Catalina's majestic kelp forest—alive with bright orange garibaldi, spotted calico bass, opaleyes, halfmoons, sea urchins, rockfish and bat rays, to name just a few. And you'll see it all from the comfort of a climate-controlled cabin.

Everything changes at night when the sea creatures who hide from daylight come out to feed. Commonly encountered animals might include moray eels, octopuses, and spiny lobster. Witness nature's nocturnal show when these unique vessels light up the ocean floor.

Tour Options	Duration	Presented by
Daytime Undersea Tour	40 minutes	Both Available from
Nighttime Undersea Tour	40 minutes	Santa Catalina Island's DiscoveryTours Catalina Adventure Tours

Submarine Rides
(Seasonal tour; operates from May to October)

Description: Take a mini-submarine ride to as deep as 40 feet and enjoy a bird's eye view of a giant kelp forests and all the unique critters associated with kelp. The submarine can accommodate two people and you even get an opportunity to pilot the sub yourself. The sub is dry and pressurized and all tours are accompanied by a trained pilot.

Tour Options	Duration	Presented by
Submarine Tour	30 minutes	Submarine Fantasy Tours

Sundown Isthmus Cruise

Description: Cruise along 14 miles of stunning Catalina Coastline to the rustic village of Two Harbors. Explore the area with a tour guide or on your own. Enjoy a sunset stroll to Catalina Harbor, a picnic on the beach, or you may purchase drinks and snacks from Doug's Harbor Reef. Your return to Avalon is a flying fish trip!

Tour Options	Duration	Presented by
Sundown Isthmus Cruise	4½ hours	Santa Catalina Island's Discovery Tours

Tour Reservation Information

Name	Phone	Reservation Office Location
Discovery Tours	(310) 510-2500	Across from green Pleasure Pier
Adventure Tours	(310) 510-2888	On green Pleasure Pier
Catalina Island Conservancy	(310) 510-1421	On corner of Third & Clarissa
Catalina Safari Tours	(310) 510-2800	At the Island Plaza
Catalina Transportation Service	(310) 510-0025	On Crescent across from Antonio's
Nature Center	(310) 510-0954	On corner of Third & Clarissa
Island Express	(310) 510-2525	Cabrillo Mole and Pebbly Beach
Submarine Fantasy Tours	(877) 252-6262	Off island reservations office (call)

TOURIST ATTRACTIONS

The diversity of entertainment in Avalon is tremendous, especially considering its mere one square mile expanse. On land, there are varieties of activities to choose from, such as horseback riding and golf. However, since sea conditions near Avalon are typically calm, water related activities like para-sailing and riding Waverunners are popular.

Though most of the activity operations at Catalina remain open year-round, some close due to poor weather or when tourism is slow. If in doubt, visitors should confirm the operating status of the activity in which they wish to participate before departing for the island, especially during winter (October through April). Following the table of Avalon activities is a listing of annual events sponsored by various groups. Although I have listed a few of the reoccurring events, new ones are added to accommodate current trends and tourist desires. Information about newly scheduled events may be obtained by calling the Catalina Island Chamber of Commerce at (310) 510-1520.

Avalon Activities

(Unless otherwise noted, all phone number begin with a "310" area code.)

Arcades			
Description: Skeeball • Pinball • Video games			
Comments: Arcade is supervised			
Name	Location	Phone	Features
Mardi Gras Arcade	Metropole Marketplace	510-0967	N/A

Art Gallery

Description: Visitors can tour through years of creative displays featuring work of Catalina artisans and their mainland counterparts.

Comments: No cost to tour the gallery • Write P.O. Box 235, Avalon, CA 90704 for more information about the festival

Name	Location	Phone	Features
Catalina Art Gallery	At the Casino across from Shipwreck Joey's	N/A	Exhibits • Annual Art Festival

Basketball

Description: Ocean front, half-court play

Comments: No cost to play • First come, first served • Must bring your own ball

Name	Location	Phone	Features
Avalon Basketball Court	Adjacent to Catherine Hotel near boat terminal	N/A	Daytime play only—no court lights

Bicycling

Description: Avalon has more than 25 miles of roads on which to ride. The various routes consist of both gently sloping and steep grades. Interior routes to and from Two Harbors are also open to riders who obtain biking permits.

Comments: In Avalon and Two Harbors, helmets must be worn by those under the age of 18. If riding in the interior, helmets must be worn at all times, regardless of age, and permits are required. Permits can be obtained from the Catalina Island Conservancy (310) 510-1421.

Name	Location	Phone	Features
Catalina Auto & Bike Rental	Metropole and Crescent	510-0111	Beach cruisers Mountain bikes
Browns Bikes	Near boat terminal on Pebbly Beach Rd.	510-0986	Rents street bikes, mountain bikes and tandems

Boating Adventures

Description: Boating adventures allow customers to experience Catalina's unique coastline locales, including secluded coves and beaches and the rustic town of Two Harbors. Guests can snorkel in beautiful coves, or picnic on a distant beach.

Photo courtesy of Doug Lord

Comments: Not recommended for women who are pregnant. Open spring to fall. Hours vary with demand.

Name	Location	Phone	Features
Catalina Ocean Rafting	Across from the basketball court	510-0211	Camping adventures ½ day, full day and two day options

Boat, Pedal Boats & Paddle Boats

Description: See Avalon at your leisure from the comfort of a rented boat. Customers can choose to rent drive-it-yourself skiffs to go fishing or scuba diving, or use pedal boats and paddle boats to cruise Avalon Harbor.

Comments: Seasonal from November to March • Age regulations apply

Name	Location	Phone	Features
Joe's Rent-a-Boat	On the green Pleasure Pier	510-0455	Power skiffs • Pedal boats Paddle boats • Row boats
Wet Spot Rentals	Near the boat terminal across from the basketball court	510-2229	Pedal boats

Camping

Description: See Page 122 for more details.

Fishing

Description: Several Avalon-based fishing boats are available for charter. Each operation provides tailored service to their angling customers, whether it is journey for big game fish or deep water rock cod. Smaller rental skiffs are available to fish the more local waters of Avalon.

Comments: All anglers are required to have a current salt water fishing license in their possession. All charter services are six-pac operations. Due to the frequency of fishing charter operation turnover, contact Catalina's Visitors Information Bureau (310 510-1520) for a current listing of fishing charters.

Golf Cart Rentals

Description: The primary mode of transportation on Catalina is by gas powered golf carts. This method of transit allow passengers to wander into the hills of Avalon and gain a scenic advantage of the bay and surrounding city.

Comments: Must be 21 and carry a valid driver's license to rent a cart.

Most carts have a four-passenger capacity, but customers can rent larger six-passenger units (as shown here) if they need them.

Name	Location	Phone	Features
Cartopia Golf Cart rentals	Crescent and Pebbly Beach Rd.	510-2493	4-passenger carts
Catalina Auto & Bike Rental	Metropole and Crescent	510-0111	4 or 6-passenger carts
Island Rentals	Adjacent to volleyball court	510-1456	4-passenger carts

Golf

Description: Catalina hosts a beautiful nine-hole, 32 par golf course overlooking portions of the blue Pacific. It is recognized as the oldest course west of the Rocky Mountains.

Comments: Tee time reservations recommended.

Name	Location	Phone	Features
Catalina Island Golf Club	Off Avalon Canyon Rd. on the way to the Wrigley Garden	510-0530	9-hole, 32-par • Pro shop • Rental clubs • Group tournament play welcome

Hiking

Description: See Page 122 for more details.

Horse Back Riding

Description: Enjoy guided horse back rides along some of Catalina's most scenic hillside and back country trails.

Comments: Age and weight limitations apply. No riding experience required.

Name	Location	Phone	Features
Catalina Stables	Off Avalon Canyon Rd. on the way to the Wrigley Garden	510-0478	1 ½ hour guided trail rides • One hour riding excursions Monday through Friday

Kayaking

Description: Guided kayaking tours allow visitors to picnic, snorkel or glide near Catalina's secluded coves and beaches. It's also way to see some of Catalina's unique marine animals.

Comments: Age limitations apply. No kayaking experience required.

Name	Location	Phone	Features
Descanso Beach Ocean Sports	Past the Casino at Descanso Beach	510-1226	-A variety of models- -Instruction- -Camping adventures- -Moonlight journeys- -Guided natural history- tours
Wet Spot Rentals	Near Avalon Boat Landing	510-2229	-Hourly or ½ day rentals- -Full day kayak/snorkel- journey to Little Harbor

Miniature Golf

Description: Award winning 18 hole course resting on a 1-acre, secluded park setting.

Comments: Operating hours contingent on weather

Name	Location	Phone	Features
Miniature Golf Gardens	Next to the Island Plaza	510-1200	Miniature golf

Movies

Description: See new release movies at the world famous Casino Theater

Comments: New movie each week. Call Visitor's Information Center at 510-1520 for current movie.

Name	Location	Phone	Features
Casino Theater	At Casino Point	510-1520	Movies and occasional music from the famous pipe organ

Museum

Description: The museum displays 7,000 years of island history, including native Indian tools, pottery & tile and jewelry. Also displayed are archaic photographs and early era fishing gear.

Comments: Cost to tour the museum is $1.

Name	Location	Phone	Features
Catalina Island Museum	In the Casino across from Casino Dock Cafe	510-2414	Displays • Quality book selection

Parasailing

Description: Glide high above the waters of Avalon for a panoramic view of the city and surrounding areas. Patrons are payed out and reeled in without getting wet (unless you request a dip).

Comments: Friends can come along for the ride if room permits. Hours vary with weather.

Name	Location	Phone	Features
Island Cruzers	Across from basketball court	510-1777	10 minute flights Wet rides

Shopping

Description: Avalon has about 100 stores to shop, including some that specialize in sportswear, souvenirs, jewelry, and antiques.

Comments: Not all shops accept credit cards or personal checks. Too many shops to list.

Snorkeling

Description: Because much of Catalina's marine life lies only a short distance from shore, snorkeling is very popular here. Snorkelers can fish feed or shoot photographs of the many animals that abide.

Comments: Snorkeling operations operate predominantly during summertime when the water and weather are warmer. Bring a change of clothing to the snorkeling site to avoid prolonged exposure.

At Lover's Cove just outside Avalon, the water is clear, shallow and rich with fish life.

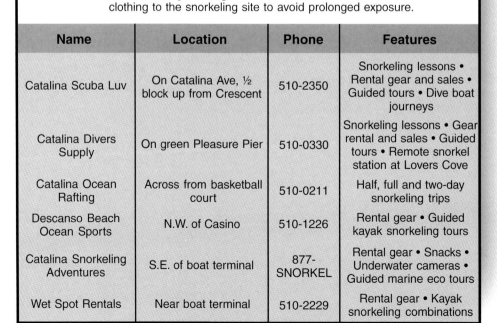

Name	Location	Phone	Features
Catalina Scuba Luv	On Catalina Ave, ½ block up from Crescent	510-2350	Snorkeling lessons • Rental gear and sales • Guided tours • Dive boat journeys
Catalina Divers Supply	On green Pleasure Pier	510-0330	Snorkeling lessons • Gear rental and sales • Guided tours • Remote snorkel station at Lovers Cove
Catalina Ocean Rafting	Across from basketball court	510-0211	Half, full and two-day snorkeling trips
Descanso Beach Ocean Sports	N.W. of Casino	510-1226	Rental gear • Guided kayak snorkeling tours
Catalina Snorkeling Adventures	S.E. of boat terminal	877-SNORKEL	Rental gear • Snacks • Underwater cameras • Guided marine eco tours
Wet Spot Rentals	Near boat terminal	510-2229	Rental gear • Kayak snorkeling combinations

Tennis

Description: Avalon has two tennis court options from which to choose.

Comments: Bringing your own equipment is recommended, although some rental gear is available at the Catalina Country Club where fees apply.

Name	Location	Phone	Features
Avalon School	In Falls Canyon	N/A	Laykold courts
Catalina Country Club	Off Avalon Canyon Rd.	510-0530	Pacific Pave Courts • Lighted courts • Rental equipment

Volleyball

Description: Avalon has an ocean front, sand volleyball court near the boat terminal, next to the basketball court.

Comments: Court use is on a first come, first served basis. Must bring your own ball.

Wave Runners

Description: A popular activity during the summer is riding Wave Runners. Riders can cruise Avalon's calm lee waters while enjoying high-speed adventure.

Comments: Wave Runners are sit down units • Jet Ski Catalina is closed from November to May

Name	Location	Phone	Features
Jet Ski Catalina	Across from Basketball court	510-1922	Wave Runners and Jet Skis

Two Harbors Activities

Two Harbors is a rustic location with lots of history. Its atmosphere is entirely different from that of Avalon, boasting a blend of Caribbean island lore, remoteness and relaxation. Its undeveloped hillsides, ocean front bays, and rustic charms have in past decades inspired Hollywood movie makers to use Two Harbors as a "South Seas" back lot for filming such classics as "Mutiny on the Bounty" and "Old Ironsides."

Today, those South Sea charms are the predominate features that attract people to Two Harbors. Though the area is civilly fortified, it remains, for the most part, undeveloped. Besides common activities like tanning, relaxing at Doug's Harbor Reef Saloon or picnicking, Two Harbors offers a variety of organized and individual activities.

Activity Inquiries

Because Two Harbors is a small, tight community, all function and information inquiries are routed through the main operations office (310 510-2800) at the base of the pier. When calling the office, tell the operator your interest, and they'll transfer you accordingly. Below is a listing of the available year-round activities at Two Harbors.

Activities

Activity	Features & Comments
Basketball	Half court play • Fees
Camping	See page 122 for more details
Horseshoes	Must supply own horseshoes
Hiking	See page 122 for more details
Paddle Boarding with Aquaviews	Marine life viewing window on surfboard-like platform
Kayaking	Rents sit in or sit on top kayaks • Kayak instruction
Snorkeling	Guided tours • Lessons • Gear rental
Tennis	Fees • Must bring own gear
Volleyball	Sand court • Must bring own ball

CAMPING & HIKING

Camping and hiking Catalina's interior can be a challenging and fulfilling experience for those who love the outdoors. The feeling of walking amongst unspoiled terrain or sleeping in a kaleidoscope of natural splendor cannot be surpassed easily.

At Catalina, many camping and hiking options can satisfy the appetites of seasoned or novice outdoor people. You may pick from civilized campsites with toilets, showers, and tent cabins down to rustic living quarters, where a corner in the neck of the wilderness is your home. Camping at Catalina can either be a family affair, a group campout, or an individual's preference to simply escape mainland crowds to become his own Zen Master.

Hiking is also a favored Catalina activity. A multitude of trails exist throughout the island's interior that range from beginning to advanced; their lengths and grades vary and are typically challenged based on your hiking capabilities and experience...the choice is yours.

Because Catalina hosts predominantly good weather year-round, camping and hiking are round-the-calendar activities. And to better serve adventurous wayfarers, camping equipment rental options are available; these are detailed in the appropriate sections.

Obtaining Hiking & Camping Permits

Hikers and campers must first obtain a permit before journeying into the island's interior. The following locations issue permits free of charge.

(Unless otherwise noted, phone number area code is 310)

Operation	Phone	Permit/s Issued
1. Catalina Conservancy	510-2595	Hiking
2. Hermit Gulch Campground	(888) 510-7979	Hiking & Camping
3. Two Harbors Visitor Services (Avalon)	(888) 510-7979	Hiking & Camping
4. Two Harbors Visitor Services (Two Harbors)	(888) 510-7979	Hiking & Camping
5. Catalina's Airport in the Sky	510-0143	Hiking

Camper & Hiker Guidelines

During wilderness excursions in Catalina's interior, campers and hikers are asked to adhere to the following guidelines and take heed of any warnings:

1. Do not disturb the wildlife. All plants and wildlife are protected.
2. Bison and other wild animals are unpredictable; approaching them for a better look is highly discouraged. Be aware that bison may charge if they feel threatened.
3. Hikers should remain on designated trails.
4. Permits are required to hike, camp, or bicycle in Catalina's interior. Hiking and camping permits are free.
5. Camping is allowed only at designated island campsites.

Camping Options at Catalina

In Avalon

Hermit Gulch Campground (888) 510-7979

Hermit Gulch Campground is outfitted with prefabricated tepees for campers to stay in.

Camping in Avalon offers visitors a chance to experience some island wilderness without voyaging too far from town. Hermit Gulch's proximity to Avalon allows guests to enjoy Avalon's daytime activities then appreciate a camp-like setting at night. The campground, located one mile from the heart of Avalon, is the town's only designated campsite.

Hermit Gulch is equipped with flush toilets, coin-operated hot showers, barbecue stands, picnic tables, vending machines, a microwave, an on-site ranger, and rental tepees. It is a civilly developed campsite and intended for families and individuals looking for campsite qualities, but desiring a few of the creature-comforts of home.

Hermit Gulch Rental Equipment

To avoid the headache of having to haul heavy, cumbersome gear to and from the mainland, Hermit Gulch offers the option of renting camping equipment. Rental opportunities include sleeping bags with liners, foam pads, lanterns and stoves. A camper need only supply clothes, food, and a propane canister to power the stove. Since it is illegal to transport propane on the cross channel carriers, disposable canisters are available for purchase in Avalon. Gear rental arrangements can be made by calling the Hermit Gulch Campground office.

Hermit Gulch Reservations and Information

Reservations are required in July and August. Various group and family packages are available. Call Hermit Gulch headquarters at (888) 510-7979 for current details.

Coastal Boat-in Campsites & Reservations

Catalina Island Camping offers visitors the option of several primitive cove campsites along the island's perimeter, each accessible only by boat. Because the sites lack camping amenities, guests must bring their own camping equipment, food and porta-potty. The sites themselves are ideal for fishing, snorkeling, or simply relaxing in cove privacy. For reservations, call (310) 510-3577.

Getting to the Coastal Boat-In Campsites

For a nominal fee **Catalina Island Camping** will provide round trip transportation to each coastal campsite. Campers should arrange transportation when making camping reservations.

Catalina Island Camping Reservations

Reservations can be made by calling Catalina Island Camping at (310) 510-2800. There is a small camping fee due upon check-in at the camping office.

Coastal Boat-in Campsites	
Cove Name	Comments
Cabrillo Beach	Reservations accepted
East Starlight Beach	First come, first served
Frog RockFirst	First come, first served
Gibraltar Point Beach	First come, first served
Goat Harbor Beach	Reservations accepted
Italian Gardens	First come, first served
Lava Wall Beach	Reservations accepted
Paradise Cove	Reservations accepted
Rippers Cove	First come, first served
Starlight Beach	Reservations accepted
Willow Cove	Reservations accepted

Other sites may be available as terrain becomes adequate for human habitation.

All Other Catalina Camp Sites

Campsites other than Hermit Gulch in Avalon are run by **Catalina Island Camping.** They offer a variety of camping options ranging from civilized sites to rustic locales. The following is a listing of campsite selections offered by Catalina Island Camping.

Family and Group Campgrounds

There are four popular family and group campgrounds under the direction of Catalina Island Camping: **Two Harbors, Little Harbor, Blackjack, and Parson's Landing.** Campers can choose to remain close to town, camp at a distant shoreline location or visit the heart of the island's interior. Each site is outfitted with picnic tables, fire pits, barbecues and chemical toilets. Excluding Parson's landing, all sites have fresh water showers.

Campsite Descriptions

1. **Two Harbors Campground**: A favorite among sea-side campers, this site occupies its own cove and is terraced from the beach up the hillside next to Little Fisherman's Cove. The area features campsites, tent cabins and tepee tents. It is only 1/4 of a mile (.4 kilometers) from Two Harbors facilities, whose amenities include hot showers, restrooms, laundry and access to all Two Harbors activities.

2. **Little Harbor Campground:** Little Harbor is a secluded site located six miles (9.7 kilometers) east of Two Harbors and 16 miles (25.7 kilometers) west of Avalon and is considered one of Catalina's most beautiful coves. Common activities here include snorkeling, swimming and boogie boarding. The campground hosts two beaches, one of which is enclosed by a near shore reef system. As a result the water off this sea side cove is generally very calm while the opposing beach is subject to surf. This varied setting lends itself ideally to sunning, surfing, boogie boarding, fishing, and snorkeling.

3. **Black Jack Campground:** This is Catalina's only interior campground. Tucked away in a pine forest 1,600 feet (488 meters) above sea level, Black Jack is nestled between the island's two highest peaks, Mt. Orizaba (2,069 feet or 631 meters) and Mt. Black Jack (2,006 feet or 612 meters). It is nine miles (14.5 kilometers) west of Avalon and 5 1/2 miles (8.8 kilometers) east of Little Harbor. Because Black Jack is in a remote wilderness, campers are likely to encounter wildlife such as bison, wild boar and deer.

4. **Parson's Landing:** Parson's landing is a remote near-shore campsite, accessible primarily by trail. It is a favorite among backpackers and day-hikers because it provides access to Catalina's rugged west end. Situated on Catalina's northwest shore, Parson's Landing is seven miles (11.2 kilometers) west of Two Harbors. During summertime when camping activity picks up, Two Harbors shore boats will shuttle campers from the Two Harbors pier to Emerald Bay, where the wayfarers then hike 1 1/4 miles (2 kilometers) to the campsite. Bottled water and firewood are provided, but campers must bring all other necessary supplies.

Getting to the Campsites

Campers can arrange transportation to any of the four campsites by calling Catalina Island Camping at (310) 510-2800. For those who prefer to hike to their campsite, they can obtain a detailed trail map at any Two Harbors office upon check in.

Rental Equipment

Two Harbors rents camping gear such as sleeping bags with liners, foam pads, tents, backpacks, lanterns and stoves (not including propane canisters, which can be purchased at the general store in Two Harbors). As an added convenience, you can pre-order your food and canisters through the general store prior to your island arrival. Arrangements to rent camping gear and pre-order your food can be made when reserving your campsite.

Reservations

Campers can book their cross channel transportation, campsite, baggage service, bus transportation and pre-order food in a single phone call. During the summer, campers should make campsite reservations at least three weeks before their mainland departure. More details can be obtained from Catalina Island Camping at (310) 510-2800.

Little Harbor is a very popular camping site due to its remote shoreline proximity. This is a photo overlooking Shark Harbor (right side cove) and Little Harbor (smaller cove to upper left of photo) during springtime.

Specialty Camping Options

Catalina Island Youth Camp at Howlands Landing

(800) 696-CAMP

This is an independent youth camp for youngsters seven to fifteen years old. Sailing, fishing, snorkeling, and water skiing are offered. Kids have ample opportunity to make new friends, learn interesting skills, and experience a fresh perspective on life--all under the direction of qualified counselors.

Catalina Sea Camp

(800) 645-1423

Catalina Sea Camp tailors their agenda to the ocean environment. Kids eight to seventeen will experiences marine biology labs, scuba diving and snorkeling introductions, underwater photography challenges, sailing and more. The camp itself is located at Toyon Bay near Avalon.

Hiking & Backpacking

Hikers and campers should refrain from walking on non-designated trails such as goat paths and rain-formed passageways . They are not surveyed and considered unsafe.

Hikers have a choice of trails to follow at Catalina. Some wind almost the entire length of the island while others are loops that begin and end in the same location. The complexity of the trails range from steep inclines to level grades. Maps detailing the island's trails are available for purchase when checking in to pick up your hiking permit. The map helps you choose a trail that closely matches your hiking experience.

The following information outlines key safety and preparation issues as they relate to hiking Catalina's interior. More detailed information can be obtained by contacting Catalina Island Camping at (310) 510-2800.

Craggy Trails: Because most interior trails consist of dirt and loose rock, there is an increased likelihood of slipping or twisting an ankle during a hike. To help prevent related injuries, hikers should consider wearing adequately broken-in hiking boots during their interior jaunts. Hikers should refrain from walking on non-designated trails, such as goat paths, etc. These types of trails are not surveyed and considered unsafe.

Sun Protection: Before heading into Catalina's interior, pack a few simple items that will help prevent sunburn and potential heat strokes. These articles include sun glasses, sunblock, water, and a hat (especially if you have little or no hair). Additionally, hikers prone to sunburn should wear a T-shirt (as opposed to a tank top) that adequately covers the shoulders. Sunburned individuals may find temporary relief by applying Solarcane or Noxema to the tender areas.

Daylight: Plan to journey through Catalina's interior only during daylight hours. Pattern the hike so that your destination is reached by sunset. Hiking the island at night is dangerous and highly discouraged.

Temperatures: While temperatures within the interior are usually comfortable during the day, evenings typically are much cooler. This is true especially for Catalina's coastal region where temperatures can be up to 20 degrees cooler than its hinterlands. If camping, carry added thermal protection in preparation for cold weather. These items include long underwear, a beanie, gloves and wool socks. If wet weather is in the forecast, bring foul weather dress, such as a poncho and a water-resistant hat.

Potential Hazards: Poison oak is a menace in certain parts of Catalina. Hikers unfamiliar with its appearance should consider wearing clothing that covers the skin, such as a long sleeved T-shirt and pants.

In the event your skin contacts poison oak, wash the affected area with an alkali-base soap such as Ivory. If possible, apply cortisone or other pain-suppressant creams to reduce the irritation. Scratching the wound will only aggravate it and possibly promote further infection.

Prickly pear cactus is another bounteous floral species at Catalina that can cause painful puncture wounds if abruptly butted against your skin. Hikers can avoid receiving wounds of this nature by being keenly aware of their surroundings and watching where they sit. As a precaution, carry a fully equipped first aid kit, including a pair of tweezers for plucking needles from your skin.

Potentially dangerous animals such as **rattlesnakes** are common on the island as well. Carry an adequately stocked snake bite kit with ample provisions for dressing wounds.

Water: Because fresh water is difficult to obtain in Catalina's interior, carry an adequate water supply. However, should a canteen or water bottle run empty, the Little Harbor and Black Jack campsites have fresh water available for human consumption.

Prickly pear cactus is found throughout most of Catalina's interior. Some of Catalina's floral wonders grow near or within patches of the prickly pear, requiring hikers, campers, sightseers and photographers to be aware of their surroundings.

Hiking routes at Catalina are diverse and exciting to navigate. However, be aware that a torrential downpour may change trail conditions unexpectedly. Below are some of the popular trails that hikers have enjoyed in the past. Trails consistent with safety and maneuverability are frequently re-routed and closed, or reopened pending safe passage. If you prefer a particular route, call 310 510-2800 to ensure the passage is active.

Hiking Routes
Reservations: (310) 510-2800

#	Route	Distance Miles	Distance KM	Grade	Comments
1	Avalon to East Summit	3.2	5.2	10% +	All uphill • Winding roads Great views
2	Summit to Middle Ranch Junction	2.0	3.2	-0.05	Slurry roads • Near Haypress Lake
3	Middle Ranch Junction to Black Jack Jct.	2.7	4.3	0-5%	Moderately level trail • Near steep China Wall
4	Black Jack Junction to Airport	2.5	4.0	5-10%	Nice views • Moderate walk Bison in area
5	Airport to Little Harbor Overlook	5.8	9.3	10%	Dirt road • Downhill Passes Rancho Escondido
6	Middle Ranch Junction to Middle Ranch	4.8	7.7	0-10%	Downhill • Dirt road • Bison Vehicle traffic
7	Middle Ranch to Ben Weston Junction	2.4	3.9	10%	Dirt road • Moderate Passes old Army camp
8	Ben Weston Jct. to Little Harbor Overlook	2.3	3.7	10%	Uphill • Near WW II gunnery Ocean views
9	Little Harbor Overlook to Little Harbor	1.2	1.9	5-10%	Downhill • Dirt road • Traffic
10	Little Harbor to West Summit	4.3	6.9	5-10%	Uphill • Somewhat difficult Dirt trail
11	West Summit to Two Harbors	2.5	4.0	10%	Downhill • Dirt trail Passes USC Marine Center
12	West Summit to Airport via Empire	7.0	11.3	5-10%	Up & down dirt trail Passes old rock quarry
13	Two Harbors to Parsons Landing	6.8	10.9	0-5%	Dirt trail • Mostly level Lovely views
14	Black Jack Junction to Black Jack	1.5	3.6	5-10%	Dirt trail • Near mine shafts 2,000 foot elevation
15	Middle Ranch to black Jack via Cape Canyon	4.4	7.1	5-10%	Dirt trail • All uphill Near farming activity
16	Bulrush Canyon Trail	7.5	12.1	5-10%	Dirt trail • A favored island hike Wildlife
17	Old Eagles Nest Trail	2.6	4.2	5-10%	Dirt trail • Passes Stagecoach Stop Hill climbing
18	Silver Peak Trail	7.6	12.2	0-10%	Vigorous • Compass recommended Back country hike
19	Cottonwood Trail	5.5	8.9	5-10%	Dirt • Moderately difficult Undeveloped Trail

DANCING
&
ENTERTAINMENT

Jazz players show off their talent at the Blue Parrot. Other establishments play music ranging from pop rock to country. Karaoke options are also available

Catalina Island is famous not only for romance and adventure but for entertainment as well. When the sun falls, an entirely new exciting ambience emerges. One may take a romantic walk along Avalon Bay, dance at local nightclubs, or relax to the sounds of piano bar music.

Most of the nightly entertainment at Catalina is intended for adults over 21 years of age. Proprietors will check your I.D. at the door, so don't leave home without it. While there may be a cover charge at some establishments, others simply open their doors to the public on a first-come first-served basis.

In any event, nightly merriment at Catalina can be lots of fun. Just find the right place, and your night will slip happily away.

The Don'ts of Catalina's Nightlife

Because Catalina Island is part of Los Angeles County, it is under the same legal jurisdiction. Laws are enforced in the same manner as that of mainland Los Angeles. Police frequently walk the streets maintaining peace and enforcing codes. Drinking alcoholic beverages on Avalon's public streets is strictly prohibited. Authorities may arrest or cite violators, and impose similar penalties to individuals soliciting confrontations. Though rarely a problem at Catalina, authorities come down exceptionally hard on those involved in this kind of activity. The preferred behavior is to keep the peace, and have a great time!

A romantic stroll through the softly lit streets and alleyways.

Entertainment Establishments

Name	Phone 310 Area Code	Location	Entertainment Information
Blue Parrot	510-2465	On the corner of Crescent and Metropole	Live jazz during summer • Upstairs location overlooks Avalon Harbor
Lady Catherine's	510-0170	Adjacent to Basketball court near Cabrillo Mole	Contemporary music on weekends • Seasonal
Channel House	510-1617	Whittley & Crescent St.	Soothing piano bar music on Fridays and Saturdays
Chi Chi Club	510-2828	On Sumner just up from Crescent	Modern pop rock • Pool Darts • Hours vary seasonally
El Galleon	510-1188	On Crescent between Catalina Ave and Sumner	Contemporary guitar Karaoke • Seasonal from May to October
Luau Larry's	510-1919	On Crescent near Clarissa	Live modern rock • Polynesian tropical atmosphere
J.L.'s Locker Room	510-0258	On Sumner ½ block from Crescent	Sports bar featuring big screen T.V.s and three 27" T.V.s • Pool
Antonio's Pizzeria	510-0008	On Crescent adjacent to Metropole Ave.	Sports events on big screen T.V. • Talent showcase where audience performs assorted skits

HISTORY OF DIVING
AT CATALINA

Catalina's marine world has attracted people for nearly 7,000 years. Native Indians, who first inhabited Catalina, hunted large fish and exploited plentiful abalone and other invertebrates from the tide pools. In 1890, after Catalina became a tourist attraction, entrepreneurs introduced and used glass bottom boats to tour the island's splendid underwater gardens. Catalina's Tuna Club was formed in 1898, shortly after the glass bottom boat appearance. The Tuna Club introduced game fishing for tuna and marlin as a sport for gentlemen anglers.

By the early 1940s, the use of diving equipment such as masks, fins and spear guns became popular. This, coupled with the invention of the Aqua Lung regulator in 1943 by Cousteau and Gagnon, was perhaps the most important development to influence underwater Catalina. Though divers seldom utilized Aqua Lungs until the mid to late 1950s when the units became more available, they did use faceplates and fins in prior years. Breath hold diving became popular and hunting was the activity of choice, due primarily to the abundance of large game fish and invertebrates such as abalone and lobster. Arguably, Catalina was the most sought after diving and hunting destination along the entire west coast.

As the sport's popularity blossomed, diving versatility expanded. Mixed gas theories were explored, TV shows such as Sea Hunt fostered diving interest, and numerous businesses sought profit from the emerging sport. With time came improved equipment technology; single hose regulators replaced double hose regulators and buoyancy compensators were introduced as mediators between wetsuits and weight belts. Backpacks made it possible to wear tanks comfortably, and manufacturers outfitted scuba cylinders with new air reserve valves called J-valves. The reserve concept helped prevent divers from running out of air; this curtailed the need to perform emergency swimming ascents at the end of each dive.

The world of skin and scuba diving grew quickly and technology leaped forward from the 1950s to the 1980s. Santa Catalina Island shared in this growth and it, too, is historically significant to the story of diving. Appropriately, because Catalina is the topic of this book, I felt it fitting to include interesting segments about its diving past. The following chapter is a compilation of interviews with actual diving pioneers of the era, who gracefully shared their stories with me. In as much as I could, the events are in chronological order with some overlapping. Remember, this is not a history of scuba diving, but rather a history of diving events at Catalina that helped make free diving and scuba diving the successful activity it is today.

First West Coast Dive Charter Boat

Though island diving, particularly at Catalina, was essentially impossible unless you owned your own boat, most breath-hold divers (usually spearfishermen) during this era enjoyed excellent shore diving at coastal coves such as those in Palos Verdes, Laguna Beach and La Jolla in San Diego. However, "island mania" entered the picture in 1951 after the introduction of the Maray, the first bonafide dive charter boat on the West Coast.

Mart Toggweiler, who worked as a civilian-contracted ship builder at the Naval shipyard in Long Beach, built and operated the Maray. During his employment with the Navy, auctions to dispose of military scrap were periodically held. Toggweiler, a gifted ship builder, saw an opportunity to make his own pleasure boat when Navy auctioneers sold surplus landing craft in 1947. He eventually purchased one for $750 and had it hauled to a rented lot in Signal Hill, California where he could rebuild it. Because his acquisition was not yet suitable for civilian use, it took Mart three years to convert the vessel into a usable pleasure craft. He called his newly refurbished, 41 foot boat, Maray.

The first charter boat to visit Catalina was the Maray, refurbished by Mart Toggweiler in 1948 after he purchased it from the Navy for $750. (Photo courtesy of Mart Toggweiler)

Originally, Toggweiler had no intention of using Maray for diving charters; however, a group of treasure divers from the Los Angeles Neptune Diving Club contacted him in 1950 to charter his boat to salvage silver from a sunken vessel called Colombia in Magdalena Bay. Unsure if he could oblige their request, Toggweiler and the group decided to take a test charter to Catalina to ensure a trip of this nature was possible. The salvage expedition never panned out, but Toggweiler quickly discovered that running paid charters to Catalina would help offset his boat expenses and docking fees.

In 1951, the twenty-passenger Maray was in full operation, offering mostly single day trips during weekends for seven bucks a head. With a full boat, the trip across the San Pedro Channel lasted four and a half hours.

Though most of Mart's clientele were skin divers who spearfished, he occasionally had passengers aboard that were experienced scuba divers. To accommodate them, he outfitted the Maray with several four to five-foot high compressed gas cylinders, which rested in deep holes he cut into the deck of the boat. Using a cascading fill system, he could pressurize air cylinders for his scuba diving passengers. About five years later, Mart furnished the Maray with an Ingersoll Rand compressor and charged $1.50 a fill.

In 1954, news of Mart's Catalina exploits reached Ron Merker, an avid diver and spearfisherman. Merker was drafted into the military in the summer of 1954 and instructed to report for duty in September of the same year. This made him unemployable, so he contacted Mart and asked to become a deck hand aboard the Maray until his induction into the military. Mart welcomed the help of an experienced diver and paid Merker $7.50 per day to act as "social director" or today's equivalent of a divemaster.

Merker's involvement on the boat did not go unnoticed. An innovative Herb Sampson developed a custom 16 mm underwater camera housing to hold a gun camera, the kind that the military mounted below machine guns on fighter aircraft to film enemy kills. Merker, who wanted to film dramatic footage of himself spearing a sea bass while free diving, eventually purchased the unit from Sampson.

Sampson rigged a mounting system for Merker that allowed him to attach the housing to his spear gun. However, he only used it a couple of times. Merker recalls, "I did most of my hunting while free diving. Although I filmed one near hit, I had to quit because I knew it would drown me. The setup weighed so much, and I had to go down so deep and far that manhandling that sun-of-a-gun was too much. I quit because I figured it would cost me my life."

Merker's true ability as a spearfisherman was challenged on a summer day in July of 1954, only three months before he was to report for military duty. While free diving from the Maray at Catalina's Goat Harbor, Merker descended to 40 feet. He spotted a large fish and moved in for the

When Ron Merker Caught his world record black sea bass, the only way to get it home was to strap it to his luggage rack on his MG Midget. Everyone stared as he made his way down the freeway. (Photo courtesy of Ron Merker)

kill. Taking aim, he depressed the trigger and nailed his target. Without assistance, Merker landed a 203 pound black sea bass. It was a new world record, tipping the scales at 53½ pounds more than the previous record.

During the Maray's reign as the West Coast's only dive charter boat, it recorded many diving milestones, particularly those related to free diving and spearfishing. One particular equipment breakthrough occurred in 1952, when Chuck Blakeslee, co-founder of Skin Diver Magazine, made a trip to Catalina aboard the Maray to test one of the first CO_2 powered spear guns.

Blakeslee rigged a spear gun so that upon depressing the trigger, a metal piercing needle punctured a small pressurized cartridge. The released pressure reacted against the spear shaft, sending it swiftly forward. Blakeslee's field test proved very effective; his first trial shot yielded a 36 pound white sea bass. In 1953, the Patent and Trademark office in Washington granted him a patent for his new invention—the Barracuda 101 CO_2 Spear Gun—of which approximately 500 derivatives were manufactured. Toggweiler himself continued operating the Maray until 1960 when financial difficulties determined its fate.

Chuck Blakeslee's very first field test using his Barracuda spear gun yielded him a large white sea bass, pictured here with his wife, Jeri, aboard the Maray. (Photo courtesy of Chuck Blakeslee)

Catalina's Submarine Diving Bell

In the 1950s when scuba diving was in its infancy, notions of touring the underwater world were almost like that of man landing on the moon—inconceivable. However, underwater tourism at Catalina became a reality in 1950 with the introduction of the Submarine Diving Bell at Catalina's Casino Point. For the first time, public access to Catalina's underwater world was possible thanks to an Inventor named Edmund S. Martine.

Martine built a steel cat walk at Casino point, which served as the base for the underwater tour. He then erected a small tower on the metal platform to provide support while raising and lowering the submarine bell. The apex of the tower contained a large tank that reportedly housed a powerful winch and air compressor. Though Martine and

Passengers experiencing the underwater world within the diving bell would likely observe beautiful kelp plants as seen here.

his blueprints have long since disappeared, accounts from island locals help tell the story of how the mechanics of his bell most likely functioned.

Using a simple pulley system, Martine drew cable from the tower winch and looped it through a strong pulley, which was mounted on the ocean bottom. The tail end of the cable was then firmly attached to the base of the diving bell. As the winch wound in cable, the submarine diving bell was drawn underwater, overcoming its positive buoyancy. To ensure vertical stability, a large steel post was attached to the tower and ran through a sealed center column on the bell, allowing it to ride up and down without toppling over. Additionally, umbilical hoses led from the tower to the bell and provided fresh air and air conditioning. Powerful night lights mounted to the tower allowed for night viewing of the underwater world.

Standing about seven feet tall, the three-ton diving bell contained twelve viewing ports near the top of the unit; up to twelve passengers stood to peer out of the windows. On the inside

For years, the Submarine Diving Bell entertained Catalina Island visitors. This photo shows the bell break surface after the winch brake was released. (Photo courtesy of SCICo)

perimeter at each window, hand grips allowed passengers to hold on and small ledges enabled children to view the underwater world. After about ten minutes of scenic pleasure, the bell would rise back to the surface, but in a most unique way. Because the bell was positively buoyant, the operator would simply release the winch brake and allow the unit to free float. Many people thought this was the best part of the tour because the bell, as it broke surface, kept on going, sometimes as high as the bell itself. A few momentous bobs later and the tour was over. The submarine diving bell operation ended in 1961 when it was removed and relocated to the Atlantic City steel pier in New Jersey.

Catalina's Davey Jones Show

Not surprisingly, Santa Catalina Island Company (SCICo) entered the diving scene in 1951 with the introduction of the Davey Jones Show. To some extent, SCICo interbred the glass bottom boat tour with the Submarine Diving Bell operation. Each unique presentation offered a marine biology discussion and an underwater exhibition by experienced scuba divers. Passengers watched the show's underwater segment through glass viewing windows.

A highlight of the Davey Jones show was the aquarium display, which operator Harold Warner kept stocked with local marine life. (Photo courtesy of SCICo)

Retired Navy diver Harold Warner, a Catalina resident, ran the Davey Jones Show under the direction SCICo. A 51 foot barge with viewing windows was placed afloat in Lover's Cove (before the cove's induction as a Marine Preserve) to serve as the base for the show. On the barge were six large saltwater aquariums that Warner kept stocked with local marine life; guests would arrive on the barge and could view a selection of Catalina's marine animals at close hand.

Also on the barge were two prop tanks that Warner stocked with marine life. After the underwater segment of the show, passengers gathered around the stern while Warner gently lifted animals from the two tanks and explained their biology and physiology. Warner recalls, "The hardest part of my job wasn't the underwater show, but keeping the aquariums and prop tanks stocked. The animals only lasted so long until replacing them was necessary. It was a hell of a lot of work."

Though the aquarium displays were unique to the Davey Jones Show, the premier attraction remained its underwater exhibition. Warner, or one of his divers, would enter the water with a handful of mackerel tidbits. They descended to as deep as 40 feet, but generally ended up just below the barge's glass windows, waving to the onlookers and feeding the fish. But, inadvertently, the excitement didn't end there. Warner explains, "The fish would wipe out the mackerel pretty fast. We started out not wearing any wetsuits; they continued to go after anything pink or red that resembled mackerel, and nipples on your breast were just that. When you're doing 24 shows a day between only a couple of divers—that got old real fast! Finally, we couldn't stand it anymore and wore wetsuits during the show." Warner worked for the Davey Jones Show until the Santa Catalina Island Company ended it around 1963.

Harold Warner of the Davey Jones show displays some kelp to the onlookers who are peering into the glass viewing window. (Photo courtesy of SCICo)

Catalina's First Scuba Program

Though in the early 1950s Catalina served as a diving playground for active divers, no organized scuba training program existed until 1958. In 1956 diver Jon Hardy came to Catalina's Camp Fox to work as Water Safety Instructor (WSI). During his reign in this position, Hardy and a few friends would combine their scuba equipment resources and dive the area's local waters, taking other camp directors underwater to experience the aquatic realm. In 1958, this casual pastime graduated into an organized activity offered to male youths staying at the YMCA camp.

Because scuba training during this era was not yet formalized, Hardy and his directors concocted what they felt was adequate training material by combining their own experience with material procured from two of the industry's first dive training books, one by diving pioneer Bev Morgan and the other by E.R. Cross. Hardy recalls, "Basically, our training consisted of harassment. We'd take the participants into shallow water then impose problem solving situations on them. Suddenly removing masks, turning off air, removing fins and administering other annoying criteria that we felt would build their skills and confidence in the water was part of the discipline." Once the divers satisfactorily completed all material they were free to dive.

During this era, divers wore wool tops for warmth, and the luxury of submersible pressure gages, back packs, buoyancy compensators and lead weights didn't exist. Tanks offered lower pressure ratings and virtually every dive ended in an emergency swimming ascent. It was all cutting edge technology, and the youths at Camp Fox endured the same equipment perils that active, experienced divers shouldered. "To maintain the safest atmosphere possible, we dictated various rules based on depth that the new divers followed. And because there were no flotation vests, we calibrated weight belts, consisting of steel weights on one inch wide straps, for specific depths—30 feet, 60 feet, and so on—to offset positive buoyancy. Nonetheless, most of the participants hung out in less than 30 feet, a common range for those wishing to take game and extend bottom times."

Diver Harold Warner of Davey Jones fame and a co-diver display the era's state-of-the-art gear. (Photo courtesy of SCICo)

Hunting was by far the most popular pastime at Camp Fox. "The divers here found that there wasn't much else to do but hunt or sightsee, and most liked the idea of bringing something back to shore with them. Besides, being a successful hunter was relatively easy. You must remember that during these early years of diving, abalone clung in abundance to exposed rock surfaces and were commonly stacked atop each other. And lobsters were practically sure catches, even during the daytime because they were so plentiful. Some of our divers also spearfished, taking white sea bass, sheephead and other tasty fish."

"I remember a particular spearfishing incident that to this day brings a laugh when I tell of it: One of our camp counselors took a group of younger campers out spearfishing from a 12 foot rowboat. While the campers remained on board, the counselor spearfished. He soon returned with his kill—a long moray eel—which he dropped into the row boat. In fear, the young campers scurried to the boat's bow to avoid the eel, but the shifting weight created problems. The tilting hull spooned water into the boat. It didn't sink because there were flotation tanks in it, so it basically became a buoyed aquarium. The eel became irate and took command of the row boat. All the boys jumped overboard. With six campers and a counselor now treading water, and an eel swimming in the swamped boat, they opted to push it to shore. They didn't make that mistake again."

Hardy and other camp directors finally received official underwater instructor credentials in 1960 after the National YMCA came to the West Coast and began offering instructor training courses. In 1961, Hardy completed the 10th Underwater Instructor Certification Course (UICC) offered by Los Angeles County. These skills together with those of other Camp Fox diving directors enabled thousands of camp participants to experience the underwater world at Catalina. At the height of the program in the early 1960s, Camp Fox certified more than 1,000 skin divers and 100 scuba divers during a 10-week summer program. Today, the camp continues to offer scuba experience options, but in a much smaller capacity.

Sea Hunt Comes to Catalina

While Davey Jones and Camp Fox entertained thousands of tourists annually, actor Lloyd Bridges stood as the ultimate diving marvel with the introduction of the hit TV series, Sea Hunt, in 1957. Suffice it to say, the influence Sea Hunt had on the public was positive for the sport. It was to some extent the pivot point for turning a technical skill into a recreational activity. Nevertheless, Santa Catalina Island's role in the Sea Hunt series was important, though Bridges himself rarely came to the island to film actual underwater scuba scenes. Instead, his stunt double, Courtney Brown, and technical advisor and stunt girl, Zale Parry, did most of the diving. Directors filmed plenty of Sea Hunt's stock footage at White's Landing because it was calm, offering divers more control over their underwater maneuvers while being filmed. Long Point and Toyon Bay were other sites used for filming small clips.

Zale Parry with Lloyd Bridges during a Sea Hunt filming. (Photo courtesy of Zale Parry)

"Filming Sea Hunt was a heck of a lot of work," says Parry. "We'd work some days from sun-up to sun-down before calling it a wrap, and for some of us the work was not always over at day's end. Because Courtney and I were experienced divers on the scene, crew members sometimes asked us to procure lobsters for beachfront dinners. Back then, catching lobster at Catalina was easy because they were rather abundant. I especially recall a particular occasion when we were elected to catch the treat. Courtney and I dived together from the rocky shoreline; I held a potato sack and Courtney filled it with lobster. I can't remember many times when I worked harder. That darn bag became progressively heavier as each struggling capture was placed in it. I literally dragged it throughout the dive. Of course, Courtney helped me haul the heavy load ashore. We got raves from the crew, including Lloyd. All were thankful for the lobster dinner." The Sea Hunt series ran until 1961.

Women's Deep Diving Record Set Near Avalon

During this same era where industry breakthroughs and accomplishments were blossoming, Sea Hunt's Zale Parry stood out as a shining Star. Besides her support role in the Sea Hunt series with Lloyd Bridges, Parry made a significant mark in the diving industry when she set the women's deep diving record on August 22, 1954. The dive was quite a production; it took place three miles from Avalon aboard a workhorse of a boat called the Weasel. Support divers included industry pros such as Phil Jackson, Paul Streate, Cap Perkins, Rory Page, Parry Bivens and more. The Coast Guard sent a cutter to the dive site to offer assistance, and KBIG radio, hosted by the well-known D.J., Carl Bailey, set up shop on the Weasel's Bridge to broadcast the event.

Ironically, the dive was not intended as a record dive; Parry planned to test a new piece of diving equipment. Because clearing water from double hose regulators was not always an exact science, about a teaspoon of water often remained in the mouth piece for divers to swallow or choke on. To prevent this, Rory Page engineered the Hope-Page non-return valve regulator, which Parry would evaluate during the highly publicized dive.

In 1954, Zale Parry set a women's deep diving record by reaching 209 feet. (Photo courtesy of Zale Parry)

The Coast Guard accurately measured a descent line and tabbed it at various intervals. Parry admits that this was more or less to make the calibrated depth "official." Crew members aboard the Weasel lowered the line and the dive commenced. Parry recalls, "When I got to the bottom, I was unimpressed. It was dimly lit and barren. All I saw was a drifting piece of bull kelp, a beer can and ripples in the sand—it was boring deluxe." On the end of the line was a slate; Parry was to sign it as proof that she made it there. She did. "The only reason I didn't go deeper was because the line touched the sea floor at 209 feet."

Hannes Keller Deep Diving Tragedy

Arguably, the most renowned diving incident was the tragic Hannes Keller deep dive on December 3, 1962. Keller and scientist Albert Buhlmann developed a secret gas mixture that allowed divers to make very deep dives with limited decompression. After a series of successful deep dive trials, Keller's experiments drew the attention of international oil companies. With the thought that man could safely reach the deep ocean floor and tap into vast resources of oil, the Keller/Buhlmann diving mixture appeared to have a real cash value.

Following a successful platform dive to 728 feet in June of 1961, Keller planned his next dive—off Catalina Island—to 1,000 feet. Shell Oil, who financed the big event, would in exchange receive the Keller/Buhlmann secret gas mixture, giving them the industry edge in underwater exploration. Peter Small, a British photojournalist and active diver, would accompany Keller on the dive. They would be lowered in the diving bell Atlantis and reach 1,028 feet shortly after 12:30 p.m. As planned, once Keller and Small reached bottom, they would leave the Atlantis to post victory flags on the sea floor. After reentering, they were to remove their faceplates and breathe the gas mixture in the bell. Both divers knew that when they did this they would pass out and regain consciousness as topside support raised Atlantis.

As planned, Keller removed his faceplate and passed out. Small, on the other hand, saw what happened to Keller and panicked, keeping his faceplate in place. At 200 feet, the support team detected a leak in Atlantis and halted the ascent. Because raising the bell any farther would assuredly end in tragedy, safety divers Dick Anderson and Chris Whittaker dived down to inspect it for the leak source. They could not spot any apparent problems, and ascended back to the support platform.

The less experienced Whittaker apparently had problems with his flotation vest during his ascent and returned to the boat exhausted and with blood in his mask. However, crew members reported that the chamber was still not pressurizing, so Anderson prepared to make another dive to the bell by himself. But despite how Whittaker felt, he insisted on accompanying Anderson. When they reached the bell, Anderson discovered something pinched in the hatch seal. He borrowed Whittaker's knife to pry it free and was successful.

Though the hatch closed, it still leaked. Anderson attempted to provide reinforcement to the seal by propping his body against the hatch. He then sent Whittaker to the surface to have the crew raise the bell. Anderson's plan was to remain with Atlantis to ensure the hatch seal didn't leak during the ascent. Fortunately, pressure variations soon caused the bell to seal itself, so Anderson ascended. Upon surfacing, crew members asked him where Whittaker was. No one knew. He disappeared sometime during the dive and was never found. Meanwhile, Keller came to and tended to Small, who was now unconscious. Though Small regained consciousness for a short time, he died before reaching the surface. Somewhat shaken, Keller was unharmed.

The dive was a success, and Keller proved his secret mixed gas formulas worked if used according to his schedule. This would ultimately set the tempo—at the expense of two lives—for future deep diving projects and milestones.

Evolution of the Catalina Hyperbaric Chamber

In the late 1960s, scientist Andy Pilmanis, with the University of Southern California (U.S.C.) Catalina Marine Science Center (CMSC), inaugurated a physiology research program at Catalina's Big Fisherman's Cove near Isthmus to study how the underwater environment effects the body. Pilmanis explains, "We were studying open water diving physiology, which included making dives to 200 feet. This was rather hazardous without an on-site treatment chamber and it put us in a precarious situation. Plus, we needed to do other research that could not be done in the water, but rather required a hyperbaric chamber. We needed to have one." The Catalina Hyperbaric Chamber evolved as a spinoff of this research program.

In January of 1974, Pilmanis found an unused chamber at the Lockheed Corporation, who ultimately donated the unit to U.S.C.. In June, Pacific Tow and Salvage transported the chamber to Catalina. Pilmanis and his co-workers then renovated the 22-ton unit, transforming it into a functional hyperbaric chamber by October of 1974. At about the same time that Pilmanis installed the chamber and made it operable, word of its existence spread; Los Angeles County officials eventually arranged to use it as a treatment facility for recreational divers.

The Catalina hyperbaric chamber being transported to Big Fisherman's Cove at the Isthmus.
(Photo courtesy of Andy Pilmanis)

Today, the Catalina Hyperbaric Chamber still receives part of its support dollars from Los Angeles County, but also relies heavily on private donations and fund raising activities to maintain operations. One of their primary financial resources is Chamber Day, a fund raising effort by which southern California dive boat operators donate a day's worth of diving proceeds to the chamber. Other support undertakings include the chamber's training and internship programs. After completing required course material, participants learn how to operate the chamber; they then have the option of participating in a volunteer internship program. Besides being on-call for chamber treatment of real diving accidents, these volunteers can utilize facility boats to dive prime sites such as Ship Rock and Bird Rock during their stay on the island.

Over the years, hundreds of people have served in this volunteer program, including well-known names in sport diving, commercial divers, military personnel and other interesting and dedicated people. Since its inception through 1995, the facility has treated 702 patients, 470 initial cases and 232 of which were follow up. Of the 470 treatments, there were 275 decompression sickness cases, 186 air embolisms and nine carbon monoxide poisonings. Not included in the 702 treatments are 165 non-treatment cases that consist of injuries requiring no chamber therapy or dead on arrival (DOA) victims. Besides its treatment success, the chamber has educated many thousands of people on diving accident management and diving safety.

The Rise and Fall of Catalina's Underwater Habitat

An artist's rendering of the underwater habitat. (Photo courtesy of Andy Pilmanis)

Another significant Pilmanis undertaking at U.S.C.'s Marine Science Center was the Underwater Habitat Program. For marine scientists to successfully complete long-term underwater experiments, they often need to spend countless hours underwater, but are limited in the duration of their stay by the scuba air cylinders. According to Pilmanis, "This was very inefficient. Scientific divers may make numerous scuba dives over the term of a project, and have to use valuable time decompressing, which makes completion of an experiment extremely time consuming." In 1980, Andy Pilmanis and Bob Given initiated the development of a saturation diving system for use by scientific personnel—funded by the National Oceanic and Atmospheric Administration (NOAA)—called the Western Regional Undersea Research Program.

"Saturation diving implies living underwater. The whole idea was that by placing a habitat in strategic locations, scientists could work for long durations and greatly increase their overall productivity. Our concept included being saturated in the habitat for up to two weeks, then the habitat would decompress to sea level. Scientists, now back in a one atmosphere environment, would lock out and scuba back to the surface."

The system's conceptual design was prepared by Southwest Research Institute in San Antonio, Texas. Pilmanis and U.S.C. then entered into a detailed engineering contract with Perry Oceanographics in Florida. Victoria Machine in Victoria, Texas built

the actual habitat structure, which measured about fifty feet long by nine feet wide. However, by the time the habitat was completed, Hydro Lab, a habitat in St. Croix, became unusable because it could not pass safety inspection. NOAA, under political scrutiny by Senator Lowell Weicker to find a suitable replacement for Hydro Lab, took Catalina's Underwater Habitat and installed it in St. Croix in 1985, where Weicker regularly saturated.

Meanwhile, during the Habitat's construction, Pilmanis and Given developed and used a "Way Station" concept for long duration dives. They utilized an open ended Navy surplus diving bell outfitted with a ballast weight system and umbilicals that led to a surface support barge. The Way Station was a mobile system, and allowed scientists to place the unit wherever they needed. The bell contained a filling station for scuba, hot water, food, drinks, and a dry environment for taking notes and analyzing data. The divers themselves wore hot-water-filled diving suits to keep them comfortable in the cold water.

The Navy diving bell served as a base for biological studies at Catalina until NOAA severed its funding.
(Photo courtesy of Andy Pilmanis)

Dive durations, unlike a two-week saturation stay in a habitat, lasted up to six hours. Pilmanis explains, "The biologists productivity increased dramatically when compared with the same jobs being done on scuba with no bell. They could collect most or all of their samples on a six-hour bell dive, decompress, then get back to the lab to work up their samples and data. On scuba alone, sample collections and tests this extensive could take weeks." Considering cost, Pilmanis and other researchers ultimately concluded that the Way Station was a more productive and economically sound system than the Habitat. Nonetheless, NOAA decided to discontinue its funding to U.S.C. and focus all their resources on St. Croix's new acquisition, even though the Way Station required only a fraction of the funding that the Habitat demanded.

Catalina Today

Divers visiting Catalina have a wealth of diving resources at their fingertips. In Avalon, the diving focal point is its Underwater Park, the most popular dive training site in southern California. Avalon is also home to numerous scuba operations that serve the diving public in varying capacities; scuba training, shark diving, introductory dives, charter boat service, specialty marine life encounters, and technical dive training are but a few of the special services offered. On the other end of the island is Two Harbors, a rustic locale also catering to divers. West End Dive Center, a full service scuba operation, offers exciting diving adventures such as introductory dives, kayak diving journeys and boat dives to Ship Rock and Bird Rock, two of the island's hottest dive sites only minutes from the dive shop. As a whole, diving support at Catalina is unsurpassed, rivaling similar operations in other parts of the world.

Black eye gobies are common throughout the island.

Aside from the actual diving operators at Catalina, Catalina Conservancy Divers (CCD), is a successful enterprise for helping to retain, preserve and study the quality of marine life at Catalina. Like other diving resorts espousing marine conservation, CCD strives to monitor, reestablish and sustain potentially threatened marine animals and ecosystems through prudently managed projects.

Formed in 1990 with the help of divers Bob Meistrell, Harry Peckerelli, Mike Burbank, Leon Cooper, John Morris, and others, CCD does not bite off more than they can chew when selecting projects. Steve Benavides, a key member of CCD, says, "We choose projects that we can be successful at, and do not take on other challenges that would exceed our resources and cause us to fail. As our financial resources and manpower improve, CCD's projects will become more diverse." Some of CCD's scientific accomplishments include the Abalone Restoration Project, Marine Thermograph Study, Marine Biodiversity Project, Kelp Growth Study, Marine Refuge Census and Research Diver Training.

CCD has about 200 members. Of the 200, about forty percent are certified research divers. The group continually strives to expand their membership base with new and dedicated divers. Conservation and management of Catalina's marine world is a much needed effort; the island's aquatic ecosystem is a fragile public commodity that is sensitive and vulnerable to the likes of El Niño and other life-altering influences. Benavides says, "By far the most amazing aspect of CCD is the commitment shown by our membership. Expansion will ultimately serve to fulfill our organization's Mission Statement: To Protect, Restore and Preserve Catalina Island's Marine Environment."

Unique marine encounters at Catalina continue to amaze divers to this day. Here, I encounter a Torpedo Ray at Farnsworth Banks.

CATALINA
DIVING OPERATIONS

Additional Internet Information
http://www.catalina.com/CDS.html
http://www.catalina.com/scubaluv.html
http://www.catalina.com/diveguide/index.html
http://www.catalina.com/scuba.html
http://www.catalina.com/twoharbors/index.html

Since 1958 when the first dive shop opened at Catalina, diving has grown to record levels. Today there are several scuba operators on Catalina that handle the flow of visiting divers. Each supports the diving crowd in varying capacities. However, good service and flexible policies prevail with each dive shop; to work with visiting divers on scheduling and other disciplines is a frequent and welcome practice. The following material outlines each operation's basic features.

Dive Shops in Avalon

Catalina Divers Supply (CDS)

Phone Reservations: 1-800-353-0330
Dive Shop Phone: 1-310-510-0330
Dive Agencies Represented: PADI • NAUI • SSI • IDEA

Dive Boat:
Scuba Cat: 46 feet • Fiberglass hull • Passenger capacity of 49, but limited to 30 divers • Gracious deck space • Fresh water shower • Private head • Camera rinse tank • Operates year-round

Dive Shop Features:
Full service facility • Open Water through Instructor level training courses • Specialty training curriculum • Guided underwater tours • Boat dives • Rental gear • 3,500 psi air fills • Full service dive station at the Underwater Park

CDS is Catalina's first diving operation, established on the green Pleasure Pier in 1958.

Catalina Scuba Luv (CSL)

Phone Reservations: 1-800-262-DIVE
Dive Shop Phone: 1-310-510-2350
Fax Number: 1-310-510-0821
Dive Agencies Represented: PADI

Dive Boats:
King Neptune: 65 feet • 30 passenger Capacity • Tanks and weights provided • Fills to 3,500 PSI • Full galley • Game well • Camera rinse system

Prince Neptune: 25 feet • 4-pak

Dive Shop Features:
Full service, PADI Five Star facility • Instructor Development Courses (IDC) • Open Water through Instructor level training courses • Shark Awareness and other specialty training curriculum • Shark diving • Camera and Video Rentals • Guided underwater tours • Boat dives • Multi-day trips • Rental gear • 3,500 psi air fills • International Dive Travel Program

Other Diving and Boat Charter Operators in Avalon

Argo Diving Services

Office Phone and Reservations: 1-310-510-2208
Fax Number: 1-310-510-2337
Dive Agencies Represented: PADI • NAUI • SSI

Dive Boats:
Argo: 25 feet • 6-pak operation • Up to 24 knot cruising speed (10 to 45 minutes to any Catalina dive site depending on location) • All inclusive rates • Divemaster on every trip

Argo Diving Features:
Instructor Evaluator Courses (IEC) • Open water through Instructor courses • Specialty curriculum such as Decompression Computer Diving and Commercial Diver Orientation • Personalized diving adventures • Guided tours for novice divers or high adventure dives for experienced divers • Photos and videos of your dive • Use of diver propulsion vehicles (DPV) • Shark diving • Dolphin and sea lion encounters • More than 40 years of Catalina diving experience.

If you enjoy smaller crowds and like to choose the sites where you dive, there are six-pak diving operations at Catalina that cater exclusively to this clientele.

Divers can arrange shark diving expeditions through most diving operations at Catalina.

Among my favorite boat diving activities is enjoying a beautiful sunset on the ride home.

Seagulls frequently tag along during the channel crossing to and from Catalina. They can be challenging photographic subjects.

Dive Operations in Two Harbors

West End Diving Center (WEDC)

Phone Reservations: 1-310-510-2800
Dive Shop Phone: 1-310-510-0303 (extension 272)
Fax Number: 1-310-510-1354
Dive Agencies Represented: PADI

Dive Boats:
Garibaldi: 45' platform catamaran • 49 passenger capacity, but limited to 20 divers • Ample deck space • 25 knot cruising speed • Fresh water shower • Private head

Sea Bass: 38' length • 20 passenger capacity • Large deck • 24 knot cruising speed • Fresh water shower • Private head

Skipjack: 24' length • 4-pak • 24 knot cruising speed • Private head

West End Features:
Full service facility • Open Water to Assistant Instructor training • Guided diving and snorkeling tours • Guided kayak dives to remote dive sites • Rental gear • Travel planning service for out of state guests • Air fills to 3,500 psi • Classroom space available for mainland instructors

West End dive shop is the heart of all aquatic activities at Two Harbors, including scuba diving, kayaking and paddle boarding.

One of West End's three dive boats, Garibaldi, is a 45-foot platform boat for up to 20 divers.

Mainland Dive Boats That Regularly Visit Catalina

At press time, the information below was current. Due to the frequency of dive boat turnover, you can obtain current information on the Internet by going to

http://www.californiadiveboats.com.

Boat Name	Length	Beam	Diver Capacity	Phone
From 22nd Street Landing, San Pedro				
Great Escape	78'	25'	40	714-828-9157
Cee Ray	65'	20'	34	562-867-9738
MR. C	55'	15'	25	310-521-9737
Westerly	55'	17'	30	310-548-6511
From Cabrillo Marina				
Atlantis	65'	20'	30	562-592-1154
From Long Beach				
Bottom Scratcher	63'	21'	30	714-963-4378
Encore	80'	25'	48	310-541-1025
Sand Dollar	66'	21'	35	909-279-DIVE
Sun Diver	54'	17'	22	800-555-9446
Golden Doubloon	65'	18'	34	888-GRT-DIVE
From Huntington Beach at Peter's Landing				
Pacific Dream	65'	30'	50	562-592-1154

Catalina's Hyperbaric Chamber

A hyperbaric chamber is used to treat several types of recreational diving injuries, including air embolism, and decompression sickness. Catalina Island is fortunate to have such a chamber at Big Fisherman's Cove near Two Harbors. Chamber personnel are on call 24 hours a day, 365 days a year. The chamber itself falls under the jurisdiction of University of Southern California (U.S.C.) Medical Center, but most of its medical personnel and technicians are volunteers.

Catalina's hyperbaric chamber, at Big Fisherman's Cove, is ready to serve injured divers 24-hours a day, 365 days a year.

Though divers never want or expect to become involved in a diving accident, it unfortunately happens. If a medical emergency occurs, the following information will provide the necessary details to contact Catalina's Bay Watch or the Coast Guard.

Emergency Marine Radio Contacts

Proximity	Who To Call	Channel
Avalon	Avalon Harbor Patrol or Avalon Baywatch	12 or 16
Two Harbors	Isthmus Harbor Patrol or Isthmus Baywatch	9 or 16
All other areas	U.S. Coast Guard, Long Beach	16

Emergency Telephone Support

Emergency Contact	Phone #
Baywatch Avalon	310-510-0856
Baywatch Isthmus	310-510-0341
Catalina Chamber	310-510-1053
DAN-Divers Alert Network	919-684-8111
Harbor Department Avalon	310-510-0535
Harbor Department Isthmus	310-510-2683
Avalon Sheriff	310-510-0174
Isthmus Sheriff	310-510-0872
U.S. Coast Guard	310-499-5380
U.S.C. Medical Alert Center	310-221-4114

Distress Message

Calling party should dial in the appropriate channel on their marine radio and clearly state into the hand held transmitter, "mayday, mayday, mayday, this is ....(state boat's name three times)....(provide boat's call sign, such as WY 2267)....(deliver distress message: I have a scuba diving emergency)," then wait for a response from the radio operator. Repeat the mayday message if there is no reply. If the calling party is not familiar with specific boat data, simply state your three maydays then provide a distress message.

After making radio contact, the respondent may ask for data about the boat: length, color, type, and the number of persons aboard. Rescue personnel use this information to help find the distressed boat faster. The information will be forwarded to the Coast Guard or Bay Watch, who'll then send a rescue vessel. Injured divers will likely will be transported to the chamber.

Cellular Phones

Call Bay Watch directly at one of the numbers listed above, or dial 911.

Experiencing symptoms after getting home

Symptoms of decompression sickness (DCS) are not always apparent until hours after the dive day is over. Those experiencing signs of DCS after returning home from a dive should call "Diver's Alert Network" (DAN) to obtain medical advice and location of the nearest chamber. Be prepared to provide the subject's dive profile to DAN's medical consultant.

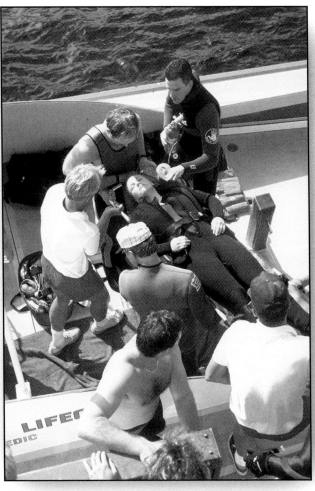

If symptoms appear critical, call 911. However, whatever hospital the patient is taken to will in all probability not be equipped with a chamber. Informing the emergency room physician that you believe the injury is scuba related and that the problem is in all likelihood a case of decompression sickness is important. Lastly, verify that your emergency room physician consults a DAN expert immediately. DAN personnel will help arrange transportation to a chamber facility staffed with medical personnel trained in hyperbaric medicine.

Though not a frequent occurrence, diving emergencies happen. Catalina's Bay Watch is always on call for local emergencies and can dispatch a rescue vessel and be at the site of incident minutes after they receive a distress call.

Divers Alert Network (DAN)
24-Hour Diving Emergencies
1-919-684-8111

DIVE SITE LEGEND DESCRIPTION

Introduction

Catalina Island hosts some of the best diving opportunities in California. To single out a favorite island dive site is difficult because of the diverse diving options available. On the back side of Catalina are several mind-boggling dive locations worth visiting. Farnsworth Banks is perhaps the most noteworthy, hosting huge purple coral-lined pinnacles, clear water and other plentiful marine species. Around the east end of the island is Church Rock. When conditions are good, this site is an excellent diving experience. You will enjoy beautiful caves, schooling fish, and many bottom-dwelling animals such as bat rays, angel sharks, and horn sharks.

Front side dive sites boast unique features worth visiting as well. A frequently visited area is Sea Fan Grotto because colorful sea fans line the site's shallow cave. Photo opportunities here are plentiful and picturesque. Bird Rock and Ship Rock, two front side favorites, are made up of walls, steeply plummeting bases, schooling fish and perhaps the island's most beautiful kelp forests. And only a short distance away is Eagle Reef, a popular site among mainland dive boat operations because of its hunting and photographic versatility.

Snorkelers will hit a glory-hole of adventure at Avalon's Lovers Cove, the island's only designated snorkeling site. Because scuba diving is not allowed here, the bottom is essentially untouched and loaded with curious sea creatures.

Diving Catalina is very different from diving tropical destinations. The cold water, coupled with kelp cloaked terrain and extra gear, can be a psychological roller coaster ride for divers who lack the necessary experience to safely dive under these circumstances. Consequently, those diving Catalina for the first time should seek an area orientation tour with a qualified diving professional. After reasonably adapting to the local environment, you'll enjoy a new and fascinating realm of adventure and understand why Catalina is a special place.

The underwater splendors at Catalina range from tiny animals like this Solander's trivia to the beautiful blue shark.

Dive Site Legend Description

The following section discusses key details of each dive site legend category. Because Catalina's diving locations are, for the most part, accessible only by boat (Avalon's Underwater Park being the primary exception), some legend categories address concerns relevant to boat diving. As a whole, the legend is intended to provide divers with a quick reference to site attributes. Additionally, metric conversions are listed to the right of each imperial listing.

Dive Site Legend

Dive Site Name

Over the years several Catalina dive sites have adopted secondary names. This legend segment lists the most common name. Where appropriate, other recognized dive site nomenclature will appear under the "General Comments" heading.

General Comments

This category describes in part useful and interesting characteristics of a dive site. Information might include its general whereabouts, commonly used surnames and other related details.

Typical Depth Range

Indicates the site's most commonly dived range. However, the maximum depth presented for a dive site, provided the site goes this deep, is 130 feet (40 m), which is the recommended recreational diving limit established by accredited training agencies. A plus sign following a 130 feet (40 m) depth listing indicates that, within the dive site boundaries, the bottom descends beyond the recommended depth limit. Diving deeper than 130 feet (40 m) is beyond the scope of this book.

When diving at any dive site, exercise safe diving procedures. Precautions such as good buddy communication, safety stops, monitoring your air supply, gages and computers frequently, beginning your ascent with an ample reserve of air, and making slow ascents should be followed during every dive, despite depth.

Skill Rating

This section is presented with the intention of defining, to a degree, recommended diving experience parameters for each Catalina dive site. With it, divers can correlate their experience level to each Catalina diving location. However, novice or student divers who are confident and comfortable underwater routinely dive intermediate or advanced sites while under the supervision of diving professionals. Nonetheless, the decision to dive a more advanced site, taking into account confidence, comfort and safety, lies solely in your hands.

The scope of these categories targets those who received proper instruction through an accredited training agency. It is also consistent with cold water scuba attire, where a full ¼ inch (6-8 mm) wetsuit and hood are worn. Divers unfamiliar with California's water conditions or the equipment used to scuba dive in cold water comfortably, should take an orientation dive through a locally accredited source, no matter how experienced that diver might be. However, it is common for experienced divers, once they've completed their familiarization tours, to dive the most advanced sites Catalina has to offer.

● **Novice:**

The Dive Site: The degree of difficulty for sites with a Novice rating is considered to be minimal. Novice sites typically provide the optimum safe diving conditions sought by dive trainers: shallow terrain, little or no current and surge, and safe anchoring conditions.

The Diver: A novice diver is considered to have been properly acclimated to California diving conditions, made up to 12 dives, have some diving experience in water as deep as 60 feet (18 m) and be in decent physical condition. A diver of this level should have some degree of boat diving experience and be currently active in the sport.

■ **Intermediate:**

The Dive Site: Intermediate sites offer a greater diversity of terrain and conditions. Characteristically, kelp, surge, current, and possibly greater depth are encountered.

The Diver: In addition to possessing all the skill requirements of a Novice diver, Intermediate divers should have between 13 and 50 logged dives and be capable of diving to beyond 60 feet (18 m).

◆ **Advanced:**

The Dive Site: Advanced sites might be characterized by deep terrain, steeply plummeting reefs and thick kelp beds. Strong current, surge and poor anchoring conditions are also commonly encountered characteristics.

The Diver: In addition to possessing all the skills of an Intermediate diver, Advanced divers should have more than 50 logged dives and taken some degree of continuing education. They must be capable of diving to 130 feet (40 m) and able to perform all basic scuba diving skills proficiently.

Usual Visibility

For the most part, Catalina's water clarity is a factor of the seasons. The island receives its clearest water during the winter months. Visibility at Catalina during this season can be more than 100 feet (31 m), but typically averages 50 to 60 feet (15-18 m).

Spring has the poorest water conditions due to upwelling and plankton growth. At times, plankton blooms and silt can limit visibility to a few feet (3-6 m), but the average during this season is 15 to 40 feet (6-12 m). As summer approaches, spring blooms begin to subside and water clarity improves to an average of 30 to 50 feet (9-15 m). Summer visibility carries over into the fall, increasing steadily as the weather makes its annual cycle back to winter.

However, as divers we know that visibility can change quickly depending on prevailing environmental conditions. Factors such as current, topography, plankton, sunlight, upwelling, rain runoff, wind and storms can either cloud the water to undiveable levels or cleanse it into a crystal-clear liquid. The figures presented in each dive site legend are annual low to high averages. Visibility during your visit can easily be much better or, for that matter, much worse.

Water Temperatures at Catalina	
Winter:	56°F to 62°F (13°C to 16.5°C)
Spring:	58°F to 64°F (14°C to 18°C)
Summer:	64°F to 70°F (18°C to 21°C)
Fall:	62°F to 70°F (16.5°C to 21°C)

Topography

Bottom composition throughout the perimeter of Catalina is a combination of igneous (volcanic) rock, metamorphic (compressed) rock and sand. Over time, geologic forces and erosion turned the rock material into a showcase of ledges, overhangs, crevices, canyons, walls and caves. Though we classify many sites as having the same general topographical traits (i.e., ledges and walls), the actual "blueprint" of a site's subsurface geology is where the difference lies. The sole purpose of this category is to list "general" topographical components for each site.

Usual Conditions

This category earmarks the most common water conditions at each Catalina dive site. These environmental occurrences include swell, surge, current and wind. Divers should deal with each of these conditions as a factor of their diving experience. If, for example, you feel that the current at a particular site is too powerful to dive safely, then sit it out or move to another location. Surge can also befuddle a dive. Though your diving goal may be to nab halibut in shallow terrain, confused and persistent water movement may prevent you from doing so with any degree of comfort.

Wind can be a thorn in your side as well. Though it may not affect the immediate diving conditions, wind does influence whether you can anchor safely. The force of swell, together with wind, can bedevil the situation further. A boat's heaving, rolling and pitching may impart sever jerks to the anchor line, causing the hook to uproot and drag. A dislodged anchor can be a bummer, especially if it happens while you're underwater. The boat can easily end up out at sea, on a nearby reef or beached. If the legend cites wind as a usual condition, it should be considered a potential anchoring hazard.

Another dive site issue to consider is boat traffic. Many good dive locations at Catalina are prone to boat traffic because of their proximity to Avalon, Two Harbors, anchorages, mooring sites or headlands. When a legend flags boat traffic as a usual condition, divers should consider it a potential hazard. When possible, descend and ascend using your boat's anchor line.

Gaging Water Movement

In areas where kelp exists, divers can gage, with reasonable accuracy, whether there's strong current or not. Simply check to see if the kelp is leaning heavily. If so, diving elsewhere may be a safer option. Another way to gage current, especially in areas where kelp is absent, is to throw out a current line while anchored. If it becomes taut or drifts quickly away from your boat, assume that the current is strong. Eddies forming around buoys and shallow reefs also suggest that current is present. Though diving in current is common and can be a rewarding experience, correlating your diving experience to the strength of the current is necessary to dive in it safely.

Surge is another hindrance. With the presence of swells, assuming that divers will encounter surge is reasonable, particularly in shallow water. To escape the heaving and pitching, divers usually head for deeper terrain.

Kelp can be a good indicator of whether current is present or not.

Featured Marine Life

Since most of the marine life at Catalina is common throughout the encompassing waters, it would be a monumental and repetitive task to describe recurring animals as part of each site's attributes. In this category, we classify routinely encountered marine life as "common" unless a particular animal really stands out as an abundant specie. For example, though sea fans are found throughout the island's waters, they are the focal point of Bird Rock, offering extraordinary scenery along the site's walls and canyons. Thus, we would include sea fans in the legend in addition to the classification of "common."

Photography

Many Catalina dive sites are ideally suited for photography, offering unparalleled scenery and consistently good water conditions. Other sites, unfortunately, have not evolved into the Garden of Eden all underwater photographers yearn for. Uncontrolled influences such as water clarity, geology and marine life, have a significant influence over the

Photo opportunities are wide spread provided you visit the right sites, such as Seal Rocks to obtain sea lion photographs.

underwater scenery. This category comments on the photographic quality for each dive site, taking into account a combination of commonly encountered water conditions and subject material.

Hunting

Overall, the quality of hunting at Catalina is excellent. Still, like the photogenic sites, there are biological, geological and environmental limitations that prevent game animals from adapting to all areas of the island. Therefore, a hunting category has been incorporated that denotes seafood delicacies, if any, that are common for each site. Animals chosen to be flagged include lobster and scallops. Because game fish, such as white seabass and yellowtail, migrate from site to site, we will not mention them as a source of game for individual dive locations. As a rule, however, spearfishing for game fish is best at headlands or along the edges of kelp beds where the fish come to feed. Comparatively, spearfishing on the back side of Catalina is better than the front side.

The law requires that hunters carry a valid California saltwater fishing license to catch any ocean-dwelling game. Moreover, hunters may only catch animals, such as lobster, during designated seasons. Be aware of size limitations and have any required gaging devices in your possession. Hunters can obtain current game regulations through a local dive store or by calling the California Department of Fish and Game at (310) 590-5132.

Dive Site Coordinates

Using latitude and longitude coordinates, boaters can utilize their Loran (LOng RAnge Navigation) units or Global Positioning System (GPS) units to navigate to the general vicinity of any given location provided in this book. The question of whether an electronic device will place you directly on top of a dive site is, essentially, a toss of a coin. For instance, the accuracy of a Loran-C unit (when it works) varies from 100 to 600 feet (30-183 m) from the target, while a GPS system, considered state of the art, is accurate to within 15 to 60 feet (4.5-18 m).

Nonetheless, whether GPS or Loran, electronic design is not perfect. Frequency variations may, in fact, inhibit accuracy from one unit to the next. Further complicating the issue of precision is the degree of error naturally inherent when plotting the coordinates themselves. Thus, the use of a depth sounder is imperative. This will allow you to sound the site, not only to find your ideal anchoring depth, but to locate the site itself in some instances.

Dive Site Highlights

This heading comments on the dive site itself. The term "no peculiar features" means that unique attributes, such as purple coral or sea fan walls, aren't part of the site. It does not mean the site offers poor diving. It most likely still contains the common fun stuff typical of Catalina.

CATALINA ISLAND
DIVE SITES

The Backside

Lands End

Map Location:	1
General Comments:	a.k.a. West End • Catalina's western most point • Very good diving when conditions offer a safe anchorage
Typical Depth Range:	0' to 130'+ (0-40 m)
Skill Rating:	◆
Usual Visibility:	30' to 50' (9-15 m)
Topography:	Wall • Exposed rocks • Steep drops
Usual Conditions:	Surge • Strong currents • Difficult anchoring
Featured Marine Life:	Common • Big sea fans • Scallops
Photography:	Excellent wide angle and macro beyond 50 foot (15 meters)
Hunting:	Scallops
Dive Site Coordinates:	Long: 118° 36' 22" Lat: 33° 28' 44"
Dive Site Highlights:	A spectacular wall dive begins in 40 feet (15 m) and plummets beyond 130 feet (40 m). Vibrant gorgonian sea fans embrace large areas of the wall and provide spectacular scenery.

Eagle Rock

Map Location:	2
General Comments:	a.k.a. Finger Rock • Looks like a giant finger sticking 50' (15 m) out of the water • Located ½ mile (.8 km) S.E. of West End.
Typical Depth Range:	0' to 80' (0-24 m)
Skill Rating:	◆
Usual Visibility:	10' to 30' (3-9 m)
Topography:	Column juts up from sand bottom
Usual Conditions:	Current • Swell • Surge • Tricky anchoring
Featured Marine Life:	Common • Kelp between rock and shoreline
Photography:	Adequate wide angle & macro
Hunting:	Scallops on seaward side of rock
Dive Site Coordinates:	Long: 118° 36' 20" Lat: 33° 28' 20"
Dive Site Highlights:	When conditions are calm, Eagle Rock is a geologically interesting dive. From a relatively flat sand bottom, the rock suddenly emerges and thrusts straight up to the surface. Throughout its vertical grade are many interesting crevices and ledges to explore.

Gull Rock

Map Location:	3
General Comments:	Located near Iron Bound's western headland
Typical Depth Range:	0' to 100' (0-30 m)
Skill Rating:	■
Usual Visibility:	10' to 20' (3-6 m)
Topography:	Steep Reef System
Usual Conditions:	Surge • Current
Featured Marine Life:	Common • Kelp inside of rock
Photography:	Generally not suitable for wide angle • Macro okay if you look hard
Hunting:	Good on inside of rock for lobster
Dive Site Coordinates:	Long: 118° 34' 50" Lat: 33° 26' 57"
Dive Site Highlights:	No peculiar features.

At Gull Rock, an unlucky octopus (with its four legs as opposed to the normal eight) swam furiously away from me as I approached it. Although octopuses are generally nocturnal feeders, this guy was out on an exposed reef surface, apparently exhausted. More than likely, his other four legs were taken by moray eels.

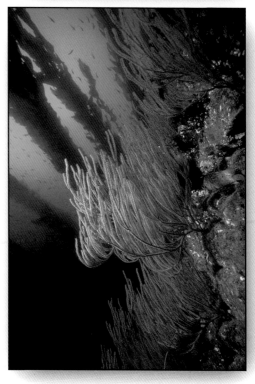

There are several Catalina dive sites populated with beautiful sea fans: Lands End, Bird Rock, Sea Fan Grotto and Farnsworth Banks and are but a few bounteous sites.

Iron Bound Bay

Map Location:	4
General Comments:	a.k.a. Iron Bound Cove • Good anchorage during Santa Ana wind conditions • Spouting cave near the west end of the bay spurts out water as surge undulates toward shore.
Typical Depth Range:	20' to 55' (6-17 m)
Skill Rating:	●
Usual Visibility:	30' (9 m) • Some turbidity due to shallow sand bottom
Topography:	Sand Bottom • Rocky Perimeter with small shelves
Usual Conditions:	Protected • Calm
Featured Marine Life:	Common • Kelp rings site
Photography:	Good Macro • Wide angle good when clear
Hunting:	Generally not suitable
Dive Site Coordinates:	Long: 118° 34' 32" Lat: 33° 26' 53"
Dive Site Highlights:	The terrain at Iron Bound Bay, along with its protective surroundings, makes the site exceptionally suitable for training dives.

Comet stars are common throughout Catalina Island.

Whale Rock

Map Location:	5
General Comments:	Rock "spouts" like a whale when surge moves in • Site lies about one mile (1.6 km) southeast of Ribbon Rock, between Iron Bound and Kelp Point • Whale Rock breaks the water's surface about 50 yards (46 m) from the shoreline, denoting its highest spot.
Typical Depth Range:	0' to 120' (0-37 m)
Skill Rating:	◆
Usual Visibility:	20' to 30' (6-9 m)
Topography:	Steep wall • Rocky bottom
Usual Conditions:	Moderate current • Surge
Featured Marine Life:	Common • Good kelp inside of rock
Photography:	Good macro and wide angle when calm
Hunting:	Lobster • Scallops
Dive Site Coordinates:	Long: 118° 33' 35" Lat: 33° 25' 55"
Dive Site Highlights:	Whale Rock's terrain is a stepped wall system made up of ledges and sheer drop offs. On the seaward side of the rock, the bottom plunges sharply to 120 feet (37 m). The site is also known for its abundant fish activity and game.

Kelp Point

Map Location:	6
General Comments:	a.k.a.: Kelp Bay • Located between Cape Cortez and Whale Rock
Typical Depth Range:	15' to 100' (4.5-30 m)
Skill Rating:	■
Usual Visibility:	15' to 25' (4.5-8 m)
Topography:	Jumbled boulders and rock leading to sand
Usual Conditions:	Surge • Mild current
Featured Marine Life:	Common • Extensive kelp growth
Photography:	Wide angle good when clear • Macro good
Hunting:	Scallops
Dive Site Coordinates:	Long: 118° 32' 55" Lat: 33° 26' 05"
Dive Site Highlights:	As the namesake implies, Kelp Point is endowed with lovely kelp beds.

Cape Cortez

Map Location:	7
General Comments:	Located at tip of Lobster Bay's western headland between Cat Harbor and Kelp Point
Typical Depth Range:	10' to 100' (3-30 m)
Skill Rating:	■
Usual Visibility:	30' (9 m) • Can reach 50'+ (15 m)
Topography:	Rocky • Wall • Steeply cascading reef
Usual Conditions:	Upwelling • Surge & current
Featured Marine Life:	Common
Photography:	Good wide angle when clear • Good macro
Hunting:	Scallops
Dive Site Coordinates:	Long: 118° 32' 03" Lat: 33° 25' 43"
Dive Site Highlights:	The underwater geology at Cape Cortez is basically a continuance of the steep rock-faced cliff rising hundreds of feet above the water's surface. As a result, Cape Cortez is blessed with a steep wall that begins in 40 feet (12 m) and plummets erratically to 120 feet (37 m).

Lobster Point

Map Location:	8
General Comments:	a.k.a. Lobster Bay • Located about ½ mile (.8 km) west of Cat Head
Typical Depth Range:	30' to 120' (9-37 m)
Skill Rating:	■
Usual Visibility:	15' to 30' (4.5-9 m) Often turbid conditions
Topography:	Steep • Boulders & rocks giving way to sand
Usual Conditions:	Strong surge • Currents
Featured Marine Life:	Common • Lobster
Photography:	Generally not suitable
Hunting:	Lobster good early in season
Dive Site Coordinates:	Long: 118° 30' 52" Lat: 33° 25' 39"
Dive Site Highlights:	Outer areas of the site may drop sharply from 30 to 120 feet (9-37 meters), creating drop offs and walls. The site's terrain is ideally suited for lobster.

The lovely kelp beds of Kelp Point attract site seers, hunters and photographers due to its extensive growth.

When in season, lobster are commonly hunted at Bird Rock, Eagle Reef, Johnson's Rock and Lobster Point, to name a few.

Catalina Head

Map Location:	9
General Comments:	a.k.a. Cat Head • Located at southern tip of Cat Harbor • Site for many Hollywood movies
Typical Depth Range:	5' to 45' (1.5-14 m) • Over 130'(40 m) around headland
Skill Rating:	● Inside headland • ■ Outside headland
Usual Visibility:	20' to 30' (6-14 m) • Turbid from sandy bottom
Topography:	Reef system falling to sand • Steep headland
Usual Conditions:	Calm • Protected in harbor • Good anchorage • Swell out of harbor • Boat traffic
Featured Marine Life:	Common
Photography:	Generally not suitable
Hunting:	Generally not suitable
Dive Site Coordinates:	Long: 118° 30' 46" Lat: 33° 25' 18"
Dive Site Highlights:	Divers venturing away from the reef and into the bleak sandy expanse may come across wreckage from the square-rigged wooden schooners Palomar and Santa Clara, which were left to rot after Hollywood movie makers abandon them decades ago.

Scorpion fish (a.k.a. sculpin) blend in well with reef substrate and sand. Because they have poisonous spines, it is a good idea for divers to look before landing, or they could be the victim of a painful scorpion fish sting.

Pin Rock

Map Location:	10
General Comments:	Located at mouth of Cat Harbor • Fed turbid water from Cat Harbor
Typical Depth Range:	0' to 60' (0-18 m)
Skill Rating:	■
Usual Visibility:	15' to 20' (4.5-6 m) • Turbid
Topography:	Small rock system • Sand bottom
Usual Conditions:	Calm • Boat Traffic
Featured Marine Life:	Common
Photography:	Generally not suitable
Hunting:	Generally not suitable
Dive Site Coordinates:	Long: 118° 30' 25" Lat: 33° 25' 30"
Dive Site Description:	Divers may encounter scattered wreckage left behind by Hollywood's film makers in the first half of the century.

Little Harbor

Map Location:	11
General Comments:	Coexists with Shark Harbor • Located north of Ben Weston Beach • Good shore diving
Typical Depth Range:	10' to 60' (3-18 m)
Skill Rating:	●
Usual Visibility:	10' to 20' (3-6 m) • Affected by turbidity and runoff
Topography:	Sand bottom • Shoreline Reefs
Usual Conditions:	Protected • Calm • Good anchorage
Featured Marine Life:	Common
Photography:	Generally not suitable
Hunting:	Lobster
Dive Site Coordinates:	Long: 118° 28' 35" Lat: 33° 23' 06"
Dive Site Highlights:	The beach at Little Harbor is a designated island camp site, so snorkeling is very popular here, especially during the hot summer months. You may also come across debris left behind by Hollywood film makers.
Precaution:	Near the entrance to Little Harbor is a high spot that the Catalina Harbor Patrol forewarns as a boating hazard. Boaters should enter the area with caution. Low tides usually expose the reef.

Raggers Point

Map Location: 12

General Comments: Located at southeast tip of Shark Harbor

Typical Depth Range: 10' to 80' (3-24 m)

Skill Rating: ■

Usual Visibility: 15' to 25' (4.5-8 m) • Turbid due to proximity to Little Harbor

Topography: Rocky bottom

Usual Conditions: Surgey in shallows

Featured Marine Life: Common • Good kelp growth

Photography: Generally not suitable

Hunting: Adequate for lobster

Dive Site Coordinates: Long: 118° 28' 52"   Lat: 33° 22' 47"

Dive Site Highlights: Excellent kelp bed scenery.

Sentinel Rock

Map Location: 13

General Comments: Rock covers and uncovers with tidal fluctuations • Located near western headland of Ben Weston Beach 100 yards (91 m) from shore

Typical Depth Range: 10' to 80' (3-24 m)

Skill Rating: ■

Usual Visibility: 15' to 25' (4.5-8 m) • Partly affected by rain runoff from Ben Weston Beach

Topography: Rocky with large jumbled boulders

Usual Conditions: Surge • Current • Swell

Featured Marine Life: Common • Lots of fish activity

Photography: Good wide angle in kelp when clear • Some macro

Hunting: Lobster

Dive Site Coordinates: Long: 118° 29' 10"   Lat: 33° 22' 20"

Dive Site Highlights: Inshore from the rock in 10 to 60 feet (3-18 m) is a lovely kelp bed and abundant fish life.

Ben Weston Point

Map Location:	14
General Comments:	Located 1/4 mile (.4 km) south of Ben Weston Beach • Diving here should only be considered when conditions are mild
Typical Depth Range:	10' to 80' (3-24 m)
Skill Rating:	■
Usual Visibility:	15' to 25' (4.5-8 m)
Topography:	Exposed rock • Jagged reef system
Usual Conditions:	Surf • Turbid • Surge • Longshore current during tidal changes
Featured Marine Life:	Common • Extensive kelp growth
Photography:	Generally not suitable
Hunting:	Adequate lobster
Dive Site Coordinates:	Long: 118° 29' 21" Lat: 33° 21' 26"
Dive Site Highlights:	Ben Weston Point is known for its abundant marine resources due in part to the lack of diver pressure and its suitable habitats for bottom dwelling animals.

Farnsworth Banks is subject to ocean currents and cooler water. This attracts a diversity of animals such as Hermissenda nudibranchs.

Purple hydrocoral at Farnsworth Banks.

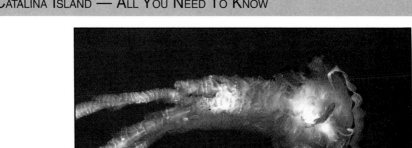

Farnsworth Banks is a popular dive spot to view pelagic animals like jellyfish. Note that this jellyfish has two medusa fish within its bell.

Farnsworth Banks

Map Location:	15
General Comments:	Located 1.6 miles (2.6 kilometers) southeast of Ben Weston Point • Easy to inadvertently end up in deep water
Typical Depth Range:	55' to 130'+ (17-40 m)
Skill Rating:	◆
Usual Visibility:	40' to 80' (12-24 m) • Known to verge on 100'+ (33 m +)
Topography:	Steep pinnacles • Walls • Difficult anchoring • Depth sounder needed to find site
Usual Conditions:	Strong current • Exposed to open ocean conditions • Generally cooler water
Featured Marine Life:	Common • Vast invertebrates • Rare purple hydrocoral (protected species) • Schooling fish • Yellow zoanthid anemones • Torpedo Rays
Photography:	Superb macro and wide angle
Hunting:	Generally not suitable due to depth
Dive Site Coordinates:	Long: 118° 30' 02" Lat: 33° 20' 38" Taken from the apex of the 55 foot (17 m) pinnacle
Dive Site Highlights:	Farnsworth Banks is a spectacular open ocean, multi-pinnacle wall dive on the windward side of Catalina. The shallowest pinnacle rises to within 55 feet (17 m) of the surface, and another to within 70 feet (21 m), but all drop into very deep water, forming cliffs, canyons, and serpentine passageways. Most dives end up between 80 and 110 feet (24-34 m) due to the steep nature of the site. What truly makes this dive is the presence of rare purple coral, which projects from the pinnacles like branching purple and blue crayons.
Precaution:	Divers should descend down the anchor line until they reach the pinnacle, otherwise current is likely to push them into deep water. Additionally, compasses are necessary to navigate out and back from the anchor line, so divers can make controlled ascents and safety stops.

China Point

Map Location:	16
General Comments:	Located midway between Salta Verde and Ben Weston Point • Chinese once held captive here for illegal smuggling into U.S. • Radio transmission difficult here
Typical Depth Range:	10' to 90' (3-27 m)
Skill Rating:	■
Usual Visibility	15' to 25' (4.5-8 m) • Usually turbid
Topography:	Rocky bottom • Exposed rock
Usual Conditions:	Swell • Surge
Featured Marine Life:	Common • Good kelp bed • Harbor seals
Photography:	Generally not suitable • Harbor seal opportunities
Hunting:	Lobster • Scallops
Dive Site Coordinates:	Long: 118° 28' 04" Lat: 33° 19' 43"
Dive Site Highlights:	The rugged terrain at China Point is ideally suited for bottom dwelling game. With the lack of diver influence on the site, hunting is exceptionally good here when sea conditions are calm.

Salta Verde Point

Map Location:	17
General Comments:	Located midway between China Point and Silver Canyon Landing • Name characterizes site as having green cliffs, or "painted cliffs."
Typical Depth Range:	15' to 80' (4.5-24 m)
Skill Rating:	●
Usual Visibility:	15' to 25' (4.5-8 m) • Tends to be turbid
Topography:	Sand bottom • Boulders • Rocky
Usual Conditions:	Surge (Subject to minimal current due to protection received from China Point)
Featured Marine Life:	Common • Good kelp growth in 15 to 60 feet (4.5-18 m)
Photography:	Not suitable
Hunting:	Lobster
Dive Site Coordinates:	Long: 118° 25' 05" Lat: 33° 18' 58"
Dive Site Highlights:	A good hunting site. Lots of fish activity.

East End Sites

Church Rock

Map Location:	18
General Comments:	Located about ½ mile (.8 km) southwest of east end light • Best dived in the fall
Typical Depth Range:	20' to 80' (6-24 m)
Skill Rating:	■
Usual Visibility	10' to 60' (3-18 m) • Clearest when surge and current are absent
Topography:	Rocks • Small caves in 20 to 60 feet (6-18 m)
Usual Conditions:	Naturally turbid from surge and current
Featured Marine Life:	Common • Bat rays • Horn sharks • Schooling fish • Seals • Sea lions
Photography:	Good wide angle when clear • Good macro
Hunting:	Lobster
Dive Site Coordinates:	Long: 118° 19' 40" Lat: 33° 17' 47"
Dive Site Highlights:	When sea conditions are sedate and the water is clear, Church Rock in an outstanding dive site. Throughout its rocky perimeter are numerous caves and crevices to explore. Fish activity is usually abundant here.

Seal Rocks

Map Location:	19
General Comments:	Located about ½ mile (.8 km) northeast of east end light • Hauling out site for sea lions • Best dived in the fall
Typical Depth Range:	0' to 60' (0-18 m)
Skill Rating:	●
Usual Visibility:	15' to 30' (4.5-9 m) • Often turbid, but longshore currents regularly sweep away debris, increasing water clarity
Topography:	Sandy • Rocky island extension
Usual Conditions:	Mild surge • Longshore currents
Featured Marine Life:	Common • Sea lions • Horn sharks • Thornback rays • Bat rays
Photography:	Good for sea lions when clear
Hunting:	Generally not suitable
Dive Site Coordinates:	Long: 118° 18' 25" Lat: 33° 18' 21"
Dive Site Highlights:	Seal Rocks is a hauling out site for sea lions, so divers are likely to encounter these playful animals here.

Sea lions bask in the sun at Seal Rocks. Hey, there's the blimp!

Frontside Sites

Jewfish Point

Map Location:	20
General Comments:	Located one mile (1.6 km) north of Seal Rocks • Named in honor of the large black seabass that used to be common here
Typical Depth Range:	20' to 130'+ (6-40 m)
Skill Rating:	■
Usual Visibility:	30' to 40' (9-12 m) • Generally clearest when longshore currents are present
Topography:	Reef • Wall
Usual Conditions:	Longshore currents • Boat traffic
Featured Marine Life:	Common • Good kelp growth
Photography:	Generally good wide angle and macro
Hunting:	Lobster
Dive Site Coordinates:	Long: 118° 18' 10" Lat: 33° 19' 15"
Dive Site Highlights:	Jewfish Point is characterized by a steep wall system that plummets from 30 feet (9 m) to beyond 130 feet (40 m). Visibility is amplified in part due to the abrupt drop to deep water and lack of sand. Jewfish Point is also one of a few dive sites at Catalina where one may catch a glimpse of the scythe butterflyfish, *Chaetodon falcifer*, a fish commonly encountered along the southern Baja peninsula to the Galapagos Islands.

Little Farnsworth

Map Location:	21
General Comments:	a.k.a. The Pinnacle • Located 1 1/4 miles (2 km) southeast from mouth of Avalon Bay • Site does not feature purple coral growth like Farnsworth Banks
Typical Depth Range:	60' to 130'+ (18-40 m)
Skill Rating:	◆
Usual Visibility	40' to 60' (12-18 m) • Known to verge on 100'+
Topography:	Jutting pinnacle
Usual Conditions:	Current • Boat traffic
Featured Marine Life:	Common • Invertebrates • Schooling fish • Sea fans
Photography:	Good wide angle and macro
Hunting:	Generally not suitable
Dive Site Coordinates:	Long: 118° 18' 27" Lat: 33° 20' 01" Requires depth sounder to find
Dive Site Highlights:	Little Farnsworth is an offshore pinnacle rising sharply off the bottom. This jagged spire is a beautiful formation of clefts, peaks and miniature canyons, and is ideally suited for photographers and sightseers.

On any offshore site at Catalina, such as Farnsworth Banks or Little Farnsworth, it is wise to descend and ascend using the boat's anchor line. This allows divers to make controlled ascents and safety stops, as opposed to accomplishing this in mid water with no line.

Sewer Line

Map Location:	22
General Comments:	Located ¾ of a mile (1.2 km) southeast from the mouth of Avalon Bay • Only one of the four pipes is active—sticking your head into it is not recommended, though the waste is fully treated • Can be dived from shore
Typical Depth Range:	30' to 130' (9-40 m)
Skill Rating:	■
Usual Visibility:	20' to 40' (6-12 m)
Topography:	Sand • Rock pile on sewer pipe
Usual Conditions:	Typically calm • Mild current • Boat traffic
Featured Marine Life:	Common • Schooling fish
Photography:	Generally good macro & wide angle
Hunting:	Lobster
Dive Site Coordinates:	Long: 118° 18' 46" Lat: 33° 20' 03"
Dive Site Highlights:	Sewer Line is a series of four sewer pipelines that extend from the shoreline on a gently sloping bottom in 30 to 130 feet (9-40 meters) of water. Three of the pipelines are out of commission and interesting to explore.
Finding the site:	Look for the rubble of rocks near the west side fence at the barge warehouse next to Pebbly Beach. Follow it seaward using a depth sounder until you find your ideal depth.

Windsock

Map Location:	23
General Comments:	Located ½ mile (.8 km) southeast from the mouth of Avalon Bay • Windsock is recognized by a modest outcropping with a flagpole embedded in it, which used to hold the "windsock" for the sea planes that once visited Catalina. Can be dived from shore
Typical Depth Range:	0' to 40' (0-12 m)
Skill Rating:	◆
Usual Visibility:	30' to 40' (9-12 m)
Topography:	Rocky outcropping • Wreckage
Usual Conditions:	Mild current • Boat traffic
Featured Marine Life:	Common • Halibut • Bat rays
Photography:	Generally good
Hunting:	Generally not suitable
Dive Site Coordinates:	Long: 118° 18' 53" Lat: 33° 20' 28"
Dive Site Highlights:	Though there is not much to see in the way of geologic formations here, just off shore of the outcropping is wreckage from a bait barge that sank in the early 1990s. The wreckage lies in 50 to 70 feet (15-21 m) of water and is often surrounded by large schools of fish.

Ring Rock

Map Location:	24
General Comments:	Located approximately ½ mile (.8 kilometers) southeast from mouth of Avalon Bay • Can be dived from shore
Typical Depth Range:	0' to 130'+ (0-40 m)
Skill Rating:	◆
Usual Visibility:	30' to 40' (9-12 m)
Topography:	Gently sloping sand bottom • Rock piles • Pipes
Usual Conditions:	Mild current • Boat traffic
Featured Marine Life:	Common • Halibut • Bat rays
Photography:	Generally good
Hunting:	Generally good • Some halibut
Dive Site Coordinates:	Long: 118° 18' 58" Lat: 33° 20' 04"
Dive Site Highlights:	Ring Rock is a series of old pipelines that extend from the shoreline out beyond 130 feet (40 meters) of water. The pipelines pass near the edge of a restricted site called Lovers Cove, but not close enough to make the site illegal to dive.

Lovers Cove

Map Location:	25
General Comments:	Located just around the southeast corner of the Cabrillo Mole • Fish feeding is common here • No scuba diving allowed • Shore entry
Typical Depth Range:	10' to 30' (3-9 m)
Skill Rating:	●
Usual Visibility:	40' to 50' (12-15 m)
Topography:	Rocky bottom
Usual Conditions:	Calm • Protected
Featured Marine Life:	Common • Typically abundant
Photography:	Very good for fish
Hunting:	None allowed • Marine preserve
Dive Site Coordinates:	Long: 118° 19' 08" Lat: 33° 20' 40"
Dive Site Highlights:	Lovers Cove offers perhaps the best snorkel diving in all of Catalina. The pristine conditions and controlled activities within the preserve provide unparalleled scenery for snorkelers. The gently sloping bottom is essentially untouched and lush with marine growth, giving it the look of an undefiled diving site.
Feeding the fish	The fish here are tame and will feed right from your hands. For best fish feeding results, snorkelers should carry fish treats in a zip lock baggie. If not, the fish will likely mug them of all their tidbits when they enter the water. Snorkelers should also be aware that Lovers Cove is where the island's glass bottom boats make their scenic journeys. However, the boats move very slowly, allowing divers plenty of time to swim out of the way.

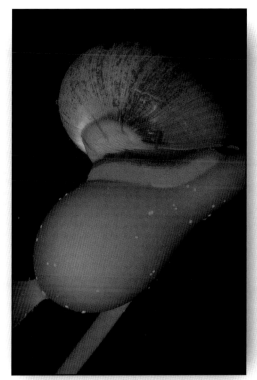

Norris's top snail is abundant on kelp throughout Catalina Island. Here at Catalina's Underwater Park where this photograph was taken, divers are sure to enjoy a good cross section of the marine life Catalina has to offer.

Divers can sometimes observe giant kelpfish hanging motionless in current and blending in splendidly with various marine plants.

Underwater Park at Casino Point

Map Location:	26
General Comments:	Located at the tip of Casino Point • Used frequently as a dive training site • Shore dive
Typical Depth Range:	0' to 90' (0-27 m)
Skill Rating:	●
Usual Visibility:	40' to 60' (12-18 m) • Known to verge on 80 to 100 feet (24-30 m)
Topography:	Rocky • Scattered reef system • Wrecks
Usual Conditions:	Calm • Minimal swell
Featured Marine Life:	Common • Extensive kelp growth
Photography:	Very good wide angle and macro
Hunting:	None allowed
Dive Site Coordinates:	Long: 118° 19' 30" Lat: 33° 20' 57"
Dive Site Highlights:	This is the most dived site on Catalina because of its accessibility. Entry and exits are via the walkway. Some areas of the park feature a couple of small boats and various piles of rubble intended to entertain visiting divers. The most popular attraction within the park is the wreck of the 70 foot (21 m) sailboat, Sue-Jac. It lies on a steep slope in 60 to 90 feet (18-27 m) of water near the park's northeastern most marker buoy. The boundaries of the site are roped off from buoy to buoy to help thwart boats from entering the park.

Valiant

Map Location:	27
General Comments:	Located in Descanso Bay near the base of mooring W43 • A temporary permit is required to dive the wreck and can be obtained at the Harbor Master's office on the green pier in Avalon • Can be dived from shore
Typical Depth Range:	70' to 100' (21-30 m)
Skill Rating:	◆
Usual Visibility:	30' to 40' (9-12 m)
Topography:	Sand bottom • Wreckage
Usual Conditions:	Calm • Boat traffic
Featured Marine Life:	Common
Photography:	Good
Hunting:	Poor
Dive Site Coordinates:	Long: 118° 19' 36" Lat: 33° 21' 06"
Dive Site Highlights:	This is the wreck of the Valiant, a 163-foot (50 m) long luxury yacht that caught fire in 1930 and burned for nearly three days before it finally sank. It is alleged that when the wreck sank, $67,000 worth of jewelry went with it, none of which has ever been recovered.

Torqua Springs

Map Location:	28
General Comments:	a.k.a. K-10 • Located about ½ mile (.8 km) northwest of the Toyon Bay pier • The terrain at Torqua Springs encompasses a very large area, extending from Willow Cove to just southeast of Moonstone.
Typical Depth Range:	10' to 90' (3-27 m)
Skill Rating:	●
Usual Visibility:	20' to 40' (6-12 m)
Topography:	Rocky • Scattered reefs • Sandy
Usual Conditions:	Moderate current
Featured Marine Life:	Common • Schooling fish • Good kelp growth
Photography:	Good wide angle and macro
Hunting:	Lobster
Dive Site Coordinates:	Long: 118° 21' 42" Lat: 33° 23' 09"
Dive Site Highlights:	Fun kelp diving and lots of fish activity at times. Look for sand creatures between the rocks.

Hen Rock

Map Location:	29
General Comments:	Located between Long Point and White's Cove • Topside rock resembles the general shape of a hen • Often referred to as Bird Turd rock due to its white guano coating • Dive boats often tuck away here when western site conditions are not suitable for diving
Typical Depth Range:	10' to 60' (3-18 m)
Skill Rating:	●
Usual Visibility:	25' to 40' (8-12 m) • Can be turbid
Topography:	Shoreline boulders • Reefs • Caves
Usual Conditions:	Mild Current • Boat traffic • Generally protected by the extension of Long Point
Featured Marine Life:	Common
Photography:	Adequate wide angle when clear • Decent macro
Hunting:	Lobster
Dive Site Coordinates:	Long: 118° 21' 57" Lat: 33° 23' 57"
Dive Site Highlights:	Hen Rock has several small caves in 20-30 feet (6-9 m) to explore.

Hen Rock Reef

Map Location:	30
General Comments:	Located ½ mile (.8 km) southeast of Long Point • Very easy to miss
Typical Depth Range:	50' to 90' (15-27 m)
Skill Rating:	■
Usual Visibility:	30' to 40' (9-12 m)
Topography:	Rocky • Jagged reef system
Usual Conditions:	Moderate current • Boat traffic
Featured Marine Life:	Common • Bat rays • schooling fish
Photography:	Adequate macro • Good wide angle when clear
Hunting:	Lobster
Dive Site Coordinates:	Long: 118° 21' 52" Lat: 33° 24' 03"
Dive Site Highlights:	No peculiar features.

At Hen Rock Reef, divers may likely come across Spanish shawl nudibranchs. A nudibranch's wild colors are merely a warning to other animals that they taste terrible, primarily due to the release of thousand's of microscopic spear-like nematocysts.

Pirates Cove

Map Location:	31
General Comments:	Located just southeast of the Long Point lighthouse • Good for anchoring and diving when western site conditions are poor
Typical Depth Range:	5' to 60' (1.5-18 m)
Skill Rating:	●
Usual Visibility:	30' to 40' (9-12 m)
Topography:	Sand • Rocky • Caves • Protected
Usual Conditions:	Calm
Featured Marine Life:	Common • Eels • Bat rays • Angel sharks • Schooling fish • Mantis shrimp
Photography:	Adequate wide angle when clear
Hunting:	Generally not suitable
Dive Site Coordinates:	Long: 118° 21' 59" Lat: 33° 21' 21"
Dive Site Highlights:	Within Pirates cove are two small cave/tunnels in 0-15 feet (0-4.5 m) of water. Divers can enter the caves, swim upwards, surface, then breath outside air that's fed through a break in the rocks. Additionally, Catalina dive specialists have acclimated some resident eels to hand feeding, but attempting this on your own is not wise.

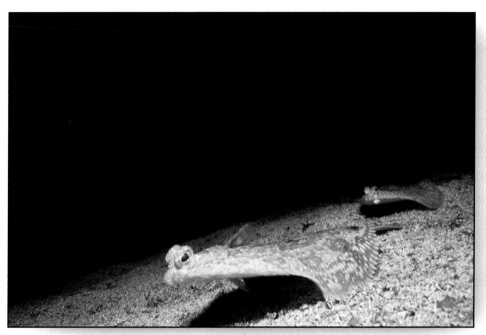

Two turbots cruise the sandy bottom of Italian Gardens. This perspective was taken using a 15mm wide angle lens.

One of the highlights of Pirates Cove are the mantis shrimp. Although they live in burrows beneath the sand bottom, they can sometimes be coaxed out for a photo with a little tid-bit.

Long Point

Map Location:	32
General Comments:	Located one mile (1.6 km) northwest of White's Cove, right below the Long Point lighthouse • Long Point is the widest juncture of Catalina, measured from China Point on the island's back side
Typical Depth Range:	10' to 130'+ (3-40 m)
Skill Rating:	●
Usual Visibility:	30' to 50' (9-15 m)
Topography:	Reefs • Walls • Patchy sand
Usual Conditions:	Unprotected headland • Exposed • Current • Surge • Boat traffic
Featured Marine Life:	Common • Eels • Bat rays • Angel sharks • Schooling fish • Sea fans in deep water • Kelp
Photography:	Good wide angle when clear • Macro adequate
Hunting:	Lobster
Dive Site Coordinates:	Long: 118° 21' 59" Lat: 33° 21' 22"
Dive Site Highlights:	Lots of animals and interesting terrain. Widest point on Catalina makes it subject to water movement and therefore, lots of life.

Italian Gardens

Map Location:	33
General Comments:	a.k.a. West Side of Long Point • Located just west of Long Point • Named after Italian fishermen who used to dry their nets here
Typical Depth Range:	20' to 90' (6-27 meters)
Skill Rating:	■
Usual Visibility:	20' to 40' (6-12 meters)
Topography:	Scattered reefs • Sandy • Walls • Small caves
Usual Conditions:	Current
Featured Marine Life:	Common
Photography:	Generally good wide angle and macro
Hunting:	Lobster
Dive Site Coordinates:	Long: 118° 22' 03" Lat: 33° 21' 25"
Dive Site Highlights:	Small caves throughout the site make the diving interesting.

Little Goat

Map Location:	34
General Comments:	Located between Long Point and Goat Harbor • Site is often referred to as Italian Gardens due to its proximity to that site.
Typical Depth Range:	10' to 90' (3-27 m) • Bottom drops quicker at the eastern region of the site
Skill Rating:	●
Usual Visibility:	25' to 30' (8-9 m)
Topography:	Sand Bottom • Scattered rock
Usual Conditions:	Calm • Eastern section ideal for escaping afternoon winds • Rain runoff may cloud water
Featured Marine Life:	Common
Photography:	Generally not suitable for wide angle
Hunting:	Generally not suitable
Dive Site Coordinates:	Long: 118° 22' 52" Lat: 33° 24' 36"
Dive Site Highlights:	Not spectacular, but very suitable for training dives.

Twin Rocks

Map Location:	35
General Comments:	Located between Little Goat and Goat Harbor • Two rocks protrude out of the water
Typical Depth Range:	10' to 100' (3-30 m)
Skill Rating:	■
Usual Visibility:	30' to 50' (9-15 m)
Topography:	Reef system with drop offs • Rocks
Usual Conditions:	Mild current • Boat traffic
Featured Marine Life:	Common • Schooling fish
Photography:	Good for both wide angle and macro
Hunting:	Lobster
Dive Site Coordinates:	Long: 118° 23' 23" Lat: 33° 25' 04"
Dive Site Highlights:	No peculiar features.

Eel Land

Map Location:	36
General Comments:	Located between Goat Harbor and Twin Rocks • Site named because it is a good spot to observe moray eels
Typical Depth Range:	20' to 80' (6-24 m)
Skill Rating:	●
Usual Visibility:	30' to 40' (9-12 m)
Topography:	Rocks • Sand
Usual Conditions:	Mild current
Featured Marine Life:	Common • Moray eels • Schooling fish • Angel sharks
Photography:	Generally good wide angle and macro
Hunting:	Lobster
Dive Site Coordinates:	Long: 118° 23' 33" Lat: 33° 25' 05"
Dive Site Highlights:	As the name sake implies, moray eels are the premier attraction of this site.

Seal Point

Map Location:	37
General Comments:	Located between Goat Harbor and Empire Landing • Hauling out site for seals
Typical Depth Range:	5' to 60' (1.5-18 m)
Skill Rating:	●
Usual Visibility:	20' to 30' (6-9 m)
Topography:	Rocks • Sand
Usual Conditions:	Mild surge in shallows
Featured Marine Life:	Common • Seals
Photography:	Good for seals
Hunting:	Generally not suitable
Dive Site Coordinates:	Long: 118° 25' 24" Lat: 33° 25' 42"
Dive Site Highlights:	Resident seals sometimes provide exciting entertainment for divers.

Kelpfish can be found in shallow expanses where algae growth is common, such as Ship Rock, Bird Rock, Rippers Cove, and Rock Quarry to name a few.

Rippers Cove

Map Location:	38
General Comments:	Located between Seal Point and Empire Landing • Good spot for novice divers
Typical Depth Range:	5' to 35' (1.5-10.5 m)
Skill Rating:	●
Usual Visibility:	20' to 30' (6-9 m)
Topography:	Sandy flats • Rocky near headlands
Usual Conditions:	Calm • Protected
Featured Marine Life:	Common • Good kelp at the western headland • Bat rays
Photography:	Good wide angle when clear
Hunting:	Lobster
Dive Site Coordinates:	Long: 118° 26' 05" Lat: 33° 25' 45"
Dive Site Highlights:	No peculiar features.

The Rock Quarry

Map Location:	39
General Comments:	a.k.a. The Halfway Spot • Located at Empire Landing and east of Blue Cavern Point • Site of old breakwater quarry operation • Easily recognizable by its austere hillside where workers once blasted away the needed rock material
Typical Depth Range:	10' to 90' (3-27 m)
Skill Rating:	●
Usual Visibility:	40' to 50' (12-15 m)
Topography:	Big boulders • Steep grade
Usual Conditions:	Calm (Its towering hillside provides protection from common afternoon winds)
Featured Marine Life:	Common • Good kelp • Rockfish
Photography:	Good wide angle and macro
Hunting:	Lobster
Dive Site Coordinates:	Long: 118° 26' 56" Lat: 33° 26' 03"
Dive Site Highlights:	Lots of nooks and crannies to explore. Bring a dive light.

Kelp is very common at Catalina. Swimming through a surface canopy, however, can lead to entanglement. Divers should reserve ample air for swimming beneath a canopy to the boat at the end of a dive.

The Crane

Map Location:	40
General Comments:	Located between the Rock Quarry and Blue Cavern Point • Named because a large sized crane once was on shore here
Typical Depth Range:	15' to 70' (4.5-21 m)
Skill Rating:	●
Usual Visibility:	20' to 40' (6-12 m)
Topography:	Rocky
Usual Conditions:	Calm
Featured Marine Life:	Common • Typically abundant • Good kelp
Photography:	Generally good wide angle and macro
Hunting:	Generally not suitable
Dive Site Coordinates:	Long: 118° 28' 13" Lat: 33° 26' 33"
Dive Site Highlights:	No peculiar features.

Sea Fan Grotto

Map Location:	41
General Comments:	Located 1/3 of a mile (.5 kilometers) southeast of Blue Cavern Point • Named because there are sea fans and caves
Typical Depth Range:	0' to 130' (0-40 meters)
Skill Rating:	●
Usual Visibility:	30' to 50' (9-15 meters) • Clarity in the cave is affected when divers stir the bottom with their fins
Topography:	Caves • Drop offs • Rocky
Usual Conditions:	Calm • Good anchorage • Protected from wind
Featured Marine Life:	Common • Sea fans • Schooling fish
Photography:	Excellent macro and wide angle
Hunting:	Lobster
Dive Site Coordinates:	Long: 118° 28' 26" Lat: 33° 26' 37"
Dive Site Highlights:	Sea Fan Grotto is blessed with a beautiful cave in 25 feet (8 m) of water. The cave itself is a room with offshoots, and daylight is visible from anywhere within. Beautiful gorgonian sea fans carpet the ceiling of this grotto. Divers can enter the main opening then exit through a smaller cavity at the rear of the cave.

Blue Caverns is a beautiful dive site near Catalina's Isthmus Cove. Walls and water movement combine to offer ideal terrain for sea fan growth.

Blue Cavern Point

Map Location:	42
General Comments:	Located at Isthmus Cove's eastern most headland • The point is recognized by a J-shaped wash tunnel that's above water • Atop the wash tunnel entrance is a sign denoting the beginning of a marine refuge. Do not anchor west of that sign
Typical Depth Range:	0' to 130'+ (0-40 m)
Skill Rating:	◆
Usual Visibility:	40' to 50' (12-15 m)
Topography:	Caves • Walls • Ledges • Poor anchoring conditions
Usual Conditions:	Strong current
Featured Marine Life:	Common • Sea fans • Kelp • Invertebrates
Photography:	Excellent macro and wide angle
Hunting:	Generally not suitable
Dive Site Coordinates:	Long: 118° 28' 37" Lat: 33° 26' 53" (Taken from point at J-shaped wash tunnel)
Dive Site Highlights:	Blue Cavern Point is a lava flow outcropping consisting of a beautiful, sheer wall 1/8 of a mile (.2 km) east of the point and a lovely kelp bed just outside the point's wash tunnel entrance. An eight of a mile to the west of the wash tunnel, in 80 to 90 feet (24-24 m) of water, are two beautiful caves, each framed below a beautiful wall system of lava rock, ledges, cliffs and kelp. Near the mouth of each cave, sea fans line the ceiling, providing more beautiful scenery. When inside either cave, the mouth is always visible.

Invertebrate life forms are a favorite attraction of most divers. Here, near Big Fisherman's Cove, corynactus anemones fully extend their club-tipped tentacles in search of food.

Big Fisherman's Cove

Map Location:	43
General Comments:	Site of U.S.C Marine Lab and Recompression Chamber • Ongoing underwater experiments around cove boundaries • Call the Marine Lab Director at (310) 510-0811 for permission to dive the site • Concerns are that anchors and divers will inadvertently disturb or ruin costly equipment and long-term experiments
Typical Depth Range:	5' to 85' (1.5-25.5 m)
Skill Rating:	●
Usual Visibility:	20' to 30' (6-9 m) • Often turbid from shallow sand
Topography:	Sand bottom • Rocky reefs • Survey equipment
Usual Conditions:	Calm • Protected • Boat traffic
Featured Marine Life:	Common • Bat rays in cove
Photography:	Wide angle good when clear • Macro good on northern promontory
Hunting:	Marine preserve • No hunting or collecting
Dive Site Coordinates:	Long: 118° 29' 12" Lat: 33° 26' 42"
Dive Site Highlights:	Diverse terrain make this site exciting to visit.

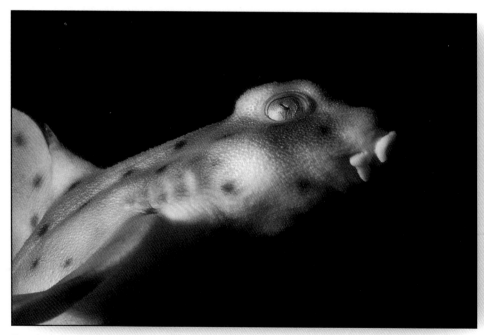

Horn sharks are commonly encountered at Catalina and other areas of southern California. They are easily characterized by a horn at the front of each dorsal fin.

Harbor Reefs

Map Location:	44
General Comments:	a.k.a. Isthmus Reef • Located between Bird Rock and Isthmus Cove • Breaks water at low tide • Approach site with caution, using depth sounder to pinpoint ideal anchoring depth
Typical Depth Range:	5' to 130'+ (1.5-40 m)
Skill Rating:	●
Usual Visibility:	40' to 50' (12-15 m) • Generally kept clear by cleansing currents
Topography:	Rising reef • Rocky • Walls • Shoals • Breaks water at low tide
Usual Conditions:	Current • Boat traffic • Strong afternoon winds make anchoring difficult
Featured Marine Life:	Common • Lots of invertebrates
Photography:	Good wide angle and macro
Hunting:	Lobster
Dive Site Coordinates:	Long: 118° 29' 21" Lat: 33° 26' 50"
Dive Site Highlights:	A favorite at this site is the wall off the southeastern most tip of the high spot, which drops from 30 feet (9 m) straight down to 70 feet (21 m).

A hermit crab in shallow water at Harbor Reefs refuses to come out of its shell, instead, choosing to peer out a peep hole just above the shell's natural opening.

An aerial view of Bird Rock.

Bird Rock

Map Location:	45
General Comments:	Located at the mouth of Isthmus Cove • Noted by its egg-shape and white guano coating • Juts out of water 25 feet (8 m) • Considered by many as one of the island's top dive sites
Typical Depth Range:	0' to 130+ (0-40 m)
Skill Rating:	●
Usual Visibility:	30' to 50' (9-15 m) • Consistently good
Topography:	Rock • Walls • Deep drops • Shallow flats
Usual Conditions:	Current can become strong • Subject to wind from Isthmus • Anchoring experience required
Featured Marine Life:	Common • Sea fans • Invertebrates • Good kelp • Lots of fish activity
Photography:	Excellent wide angle and macro
Hunting:	Lobster
Dive Site Coordinates:	Long: 118° 29' 12" Lat: 33° 27' 04"
Dive Site Highlights:	In close to the rock at the northwest region lies a shallow gorgonian-covered wall in 10 to 35 feet (3-10.5 m). The outer expanse of this zone transforms into rifts and valleys, creating a playground of huge ledges and canyons in 20 to 80 feet (6-24 m). The primary highlight of the eastern region is its spectacular wall beginning in 20 feet (6 m) and plunging to a rock bottom at 120 feet (37 m). Remaining areas are a combination of cascading ledges and talus terrain.

One highlight of Bird Rock is the number of invertebrates it hosts. Here, a spiral-gilled tube worm fully extends it frilly appendages to catch drifting food particles.

Isthmus High Spot

Map Location:	46
General Comments:	Located between Bird Rock and Ship Rock • Anchoring experience required
Typical Depth Range:	40' to 130' (12-40 m) • A depth sounder is required to find the reef
Skill Rating:	◆
Usual Visibility:	40' to 50' (12-15 m)
Topography:	Rocky reef
Usual Conditions:	Current (especially strong during tidal changes) • Boat traffic
Featured Marine Life:	Common • Invertebrates
Photography:	Good Macro
Hunting:	Adequate for scallops
Dive Site Coordinates:	Long: 118° 29' 21" Lat: 33° 27' 15"
Dive Site Highlights:	Over a broad expanse, the rocky terrain cascades erratically to humpbacking peaks, cracks, and ledges encrusted with beautiful macro photo subjects.

Ship Rock's surrounding kelp bed is one of the thickest on Catalina.

Ship Rock.

Ship Rock

Map Location:	47
General Comments:	Located just under one mile (1.6 km) northwest of Bird Rock • Ship Rock juts 70 feet (21 m) out of the water • Navigational light on apex of rock • Considered by many as the best dive on the front side of the island
Typical Depth Range:	10' to 130' (3-40 m)
Skill Rating:	■
Usual Visibility:	40' to 60' (12-18 m)
Topography:	Steep rock • Ledges
Usual Conditions:	Subject to strong current • Subject to wind from Isthmus • Surge • Anchoring experience required
Featured Marine Life:	Common • Schooling fish • Thick kelp grows as deep as 80 feet (24 m) • Yellow colonial anemones • Sea fans
Photography:	Excellent macro and wide angle • Ship Rock's consistently good visibility, coupled with a potpourri of magnificent marine life makes it an exceptional photographic splendor
Hunting:	Lobster and Scallops
Dive Site Coordinates:	Long: 118° 29' 30" Lat: 33° 27' 47"
Dive Site Highlights:	Scenic Ship Rock consists of steeply sloping terrain that leads to deep water. The picturesque scenery along the many contours is rich in content and quality. A beautiful kelp bed surrounds the rock and is accented by current-swept water, which attracts enormous schools of blacksmith. In shallow water near the southern section of Ship Rock (15 feet or 5 m) lies the scattered remains of the Diosa del Mar, a 90-year-old sailing schooner that crashed into the shallow reef here in 1989.

Lion Head

Map Location:	48
General Comments:	Located at the western headland of Cherry Cove • Named because a rock there at one time resembled a lion's head until erosion crippled it
Typical Depth Range:	10' to 60' (3-18 m)
Skill Rating:	●
Usual Visibility:	30' to 40' (9-12 m)
Topography:	Rocky • Sandy shoals • scattered reefs • Large cavities
Usual Conditions:	Calm • Protected • Boat traffic • Lion Head is shielded from common afternoon winds, offering adequate anchoring and diving conditions in the afternoon
Featured Marine Life:	Common
Photography:	Good wide angle when clear
Hunting:	Generally not suitable
Dive Site Coordinates:	Long: 118° 30' 04" Lat: 33° 27' 11"
Dive Site Highlights:	No peculiar features.

Mats of yellow colonial zoanthid anemones inhabit sites such as Ship Rock, Little Farnsworth and Farnsworth Banks, where current is typically present.

A male kelp crab (the large red crab) embraces its female mate (the smaller dark purple one) as a protective jester due to my presence.

Not withstanding the periodic effects of El Niño, kelp growth is very abundant at Eagle Reef and a favorite among underwater photographers, hunters and sight-seers.

Eagle Reef

Map Location:	49
General Comments:	Located less than ½ of a mile (.8 km) northwest of Lion Head • Composed of three mounts • Eastern peak is marked with a Red navigational buoy
Typical Depth Range:	5' to 130'+ (1.5-40 m)
Skill Rating:	◆
Usual Visibility:	40' to 60' (12-18 m) • Generally kept clean by current
Topography:	Pyramiding reef • Sand patches • Overhangs
Usual Conditions:	Offshore currents (If kelp is leaning heavily on a horizontal plane, diving elsewhere may be best)
Featured Marine Life:	Common • Typically abundant • Extensive kelp
Photography:	Excellent wide angle & macro
Hunting:	Lobster
Dive Site Coordinates:	Long: 118° 30' 25" Lat: 33° 27' 37"
Dive Site Highlights:	Eagle Reef offers exciting diving on either of its three offshore mounts. The peaks themselves are beautiful pyramiding systems of ledges, small cliffs and plateaus. And due to the site's extensive kelp growth and frequently clear visibility, it is a favorite among underwater photographers.

Eel Cove

Map Location:	50
General Comments:	Located between Lions Head and Howland's Landing
Typical Depth Range:	5' to 30' (1.5-9 m)
Skill Rating:	●
Usual Visibility:	25' to 35' (8-10.5 m)
Topography:	Sandy • Scattered reefs • Rocky
Usual Conditions:	Mild current • Surge
Featured Marine Life:	Common
Photography:	Good for moray eels
Hunting:	Lobster
Dive Site Coordinates:	Long: 118° 30' 42" Lat: 33° 27' 21"
Dive Site Highlights:	The multitude of reef cavities, honed by millions of years of water movement, provide good habitats for moray eels.

Little Geiger

Map Location:	51
General Comments:	Located between Howland's Landing and Lion Head • Dependable alternative for a final dive of the day • Good training site
Typical Depth Range:	5' to 25' (1.5-8 m)
Skill Rating:	●
Usual Visibility:	25' to 35' (8-10.5 m) • Often turbid
Topography:	Jumbled rock • Scattered reef • Sandy shoals
Usual Conditions:	Calm • Protected • Good anchorage
Featured Marine Life:	Common
Photography:	Generally poor
Hunting:	Generally not suitable
Dive Site Coordinates:	Long: 118° 30' 55" Lat: 33° 27' 27"
Dive Site Highlights:	No peculiar features.

Big Geiger

Map Location:	52
General Comments:	Located between Howland's Landing and Lion Head • Good alternative for a final dive of the day • Good training site
Typical Depth Range:	5' to 25' (1.5-8 m)
Skill Rating:	●
Usual Visibility:	25' to 35' (8-10.5 m)
Topography:	Jumbled rock • Scattered reef • Sandy shoals
Usual Conditions:	Calm • Protected cove
Featured Marine Life:	Common
Photography:	Generally poor
Hunting:	Some lobster
Dive Site Coordinates:	Long: 118° 31' 05" Lat: 33° 27' 33"
Dive Site Highlights:	No peculiar features.

Indian Rock in Emerald Bay

Map Location:	53
General Comments:	Located between Arrow Point and Emerald Bay, approximately 250 yards (228 m) off shore
Typical Depth Range:	10' to 80' (3-24 m)
Skill Rating:	●
Usual Visibility:	20' to 40' (6-12 m)
Topography:	Rocky reef • Ledges • Sandy • Rock covers and uncovers with tidal fluctuations
Usual Conditions:	Generally calm • Arrow Point headland helps to protect site from wind and swell activity
Featured Marine Life:	Common • Good kelp
Photography:	Good wide angle when clear • Macro good
Hunting:	Lobster
Dive Site Coordinates:	Long: 118° 31' 31" Lat: 33° 28' 05"
Dive Site Highlights:	Emerald Bay's Indian Rock is a fabulous dive site consisting of generally clear water and calm environmental conditions. The reef's vertical dimension is like that of a defective pyramid, dropping sporadically to a sandy bottom in 80 feet (24 meters). Its contours embody a montage of juxtaposed shelves, overhangs, cavities and shoals, each providing habitats for a vast array of aquatic critters.

Painted Greenling on a shallow ledge at Indian Rock. Note how these cryptic animals blend in so well with their surroundings.

Parson's Landing

Map Location:	54
General Comments:	Located between Stony Point and Arrow Point
Typical Depth Range:	5' to 60' (1.5-18 m)
Skill Rating:	●
Usual Visibility:	25' to 35' (8-10.5 m)
Topography:	Rocks • Reefs • Sand
Usual Conditions:	Calm • Good anchorage due to protection it receives from Stony Point
Featured Marine Life:	Common • Diverse
Photography:	Generally good wide angle and macro
Hunting:	Lobster
Dive Site Coordinates:	Long: 118° 32' 58" Lat: 33° 28' 27"
Dive Site Highlights:	No peculiar features.

Black Point

Map Location:	55
General Comments:	a.k.a. Black Rock • Located between Johnson's Rock and Parson's Landing • Site is characterized by a dark hued shoreline rock that Juts some 60 to 70 feet (18-21 m) out of the water.
Typical Depth Range:	20' to 120' (6-37 m)
Skill Rating:	●
Usual Visibility:	30' to 40' (9-12 m)
Topography:	Jagged reefs • Jumbled rocks
Usual Conditions:	Exposed • Current • Surge • Wind
Featured Marine Life:	Common • Beautiful sea fan growth
Photography:	Good for sea fans, schooling fish and invertebrates
Hunting:	Lobster • Scallops
Dive Site Coordinates:	Long: 118° 34' 44" Lat: 33° 28' 33"
Dive Site Highlights:	Black Point is an excellent site for hunting scallops. There's also colorful sea fan scenery throughout the 90 to 120 foot (27-37 m) expanse.

Due to Black Point's exposure to open ocean, invertebrate life here is teeming. Colorful tube worms are common, but approaching them for a photograph takes time and extreme patience.

Johnson's Rocks

Map Location:	56
General Comments:	Located between Lands End and Black Rock • Site characterized by two reefs that break the surface approximately 100 yards (91 m) and 250 yards (227 m) from shore.
Typical Depth Range:	10' to 90' (3-27 m)
Skill Rating:	●
Usual Visibility:	20' to 40' (6-12 m)
Topography:	Enormous jumbled rocks • Scattered reefs
Usual Conditions:	Current • Surge in shallows • Wind
Featured Marine Life:	Common • Nudibranchs • Thick kelp • Schooling fish
Photography:	Good wide angle when clear • Macro good
Hunting:	Lobster in shallows • Scallops
Dive Site Coordinates:	Long: 118° 35' 22" Lat: 33° 28' 39"
Dive Site Highlights:	Surrounding the site's two protruding rocks is a massive reef system, interspersed with huge jumbled boulders, large rock piles and sand flats. This terrain cascades intermittently to the sand bottom at 90 feet (27 meters), but the site's best scenery is found in 40 to 70 feet (12-21 meters).

The terrain comprising Johnson's Rock varies from scattered reefs and ledges to flat, talus areas. On the outer extremes of the site, reef drop offs are common, so divers are likely to come across large sea fans swaying to the pulse of passing water.

Dive Site Maps

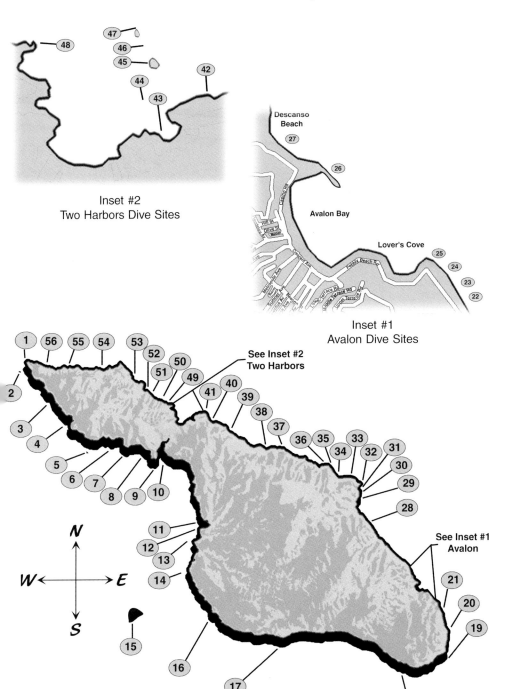

Inset #2
Two Harbors Dive Sites

Descanso Beach

Avalon Bay

Lover's Cove

Inset #1
Avalon Dive Sites

See Inset #2
Two Harbors

See Inset #1
Avalon

N
W → E
S

MARINE LIFE

With few exceptions, the marine life at Catalina is common to the islands of Southern California. For instance, garibaldi are widespread. Divers are likely to cross paths with these animals despite what island they're diving. On the other hand, some dive locations are earmarked by unique marine attributes. This is easily illustrated by the purple coral found at Catalina's Farnsworth Banks. Here, the site embodies a magnificent montage of purple and blue hydrocoral in its densest form, a trait uncommon of other Catalina dive sites.

Divers new to California's underwater world will find that, as a whole, the web of life is beautiful and fascinating. However, some marine species occupying these waters can inflict serious injuries to unwary divers. Frankly, most aquatic injuries are the fault of the diver, not the animal — that is, an animal unintentionally provoked by an elbow or knee will likely inflict injury to protect its well-being. Thus, at any new diving region, aquanauts should first acquaint themselves with the web of animals that awaits them. Familiarity with local marine life can aid in the prevention of animal-inflicted injuries most of the time. The following section describes potentially unsafe marine denizens encountered at Catalina.

Potentially Dangerous Marinelife

Kelp:
Perhaps the principal reason for visiting Catalina's underwater world is to see the beautiful, emerald-green kelp forests. However, the fear inherent in many divers new to kelp diving is that it will reach out and "grab" them. Of course, this is not true. The most common kelp quandary is that it is stringy and can easily tangle in a fin buckle, tank valve or other gear. If this happens, the key is to not panic. Do not start twisting and turning. Simply reach for the entangled kelp and break it. Kelp is brittle and snaps very easily. Sometimes a good "yank" will do the trick. If all else fails, use your knife.

Sea Urchins:
Sea urchins are round, reef-dwelling animals with numerous lengthy spines protruding from their shells. Where there is kelp, sea urchins are likely in the area because they find this giant plant delicious. Consequently, they are largely responsible for destroying kelp bed communities.

However, divers should be concerned with puncture wounds. Those with poor buoyancy control become unbalanced and often find themselves fending a reef with their elbows, hands or knees. Sometimes, divers make contact with a sea urchin and a spine or two is broken off into their skin. If this happens to you, clean the area of contact with an antibiotic solution. You may attempt to remove the broken spine with tweezers, but be aware that the calcified debris is brittle and crumbles easily. Sometimes it is necessary to wait until the area festers up and the spine works its way out.

Scorpionfish:
Scorpionfish are reef-dwelling animals with excellent cryptic abilities. They also possess venomous dorsal and anal fin spines, which, if contacted, can puncture a diver's skin, producing pain and irritation. Contact with this animal is uncommon, but can occur when divers with poor buoyancy control inadvertently land on one. Divers getting stung should immerse the wound in hot water (120°F/49°C) for 30 minutes to neutralize the venom. Consult a physician as soon as possible.

Stingray: Stingrays have a barbed spine located midway between the tail and body. Because these animals reside almost exclusively on sandy terrain, divers encounter them more frequently during beach dives. Nearly all stingray injuries result from divers stepping on one during a beach entry or exit. To avoid being "zapped", shuffle your feet as opposed to walking. This technique usually frightens the animal away before a diver can step on it. In the event of a stingray barb laceration, clean all debris from the wound and wash it with an antibiotic solution. Immerse the wound in hot water (120°F/49°C) for 30 minutes to neutralize the venom. Consult a physician immediately. Stingray wounds of the California species are not fatal but very painful.

Electric Ray: Injuries from electric rays are an infrequent occurrence, but they can present problems if divers are not careful. The electric ray emits a powerful electric shock that can stun prey and fend off aggressive animals, including divers. Approach this animal with caution. Better yet, just observe and avoid a potentially shocking experience.

Moray Eels: California morays are common reef-dwelling eels that hide in holes and crevices. Their needle-like teeth help to capture target prey such as octopus, but these sharp appendages can also inflict serious lacerations to a diver's hand or fingers. Though not typically aggressive toward divers, morays are known to attack when provoked; divers seeking lobster and abalone should first illuminate the cavity they're reaching into to ensure it is unoccupied by a moray. If bitten, victims should exit the water, rinse the injured area with an antibiotic solution, apply a pressure dressing and get to a hospital for further evaluation.

Seals & Sea Lions: Basically, seals and sea lions (pinnipeds) pose little threat to divers. In fact, watching them frolic underwater is a fabulous experience. Concerns as they relate to divers arise when the pinnipeds perform their acrobatics at arm's length. If a diver maneuvers to pet one, the animal may sense aggression and inflict a nasty bite, similar to what a dog might administer. With pinniped pups, a move to caress them might result in a visit from a protective bull who'll likely charge, coming to within inches of sending you to the moon. To avoid potential conflicts, don't touch! Just enjoy the show. However, should a diver be bitten, treat the wound by rinsing it with an antibiotic solution, then apply a pressure dressing to stop the bleeding. Victims should seek further medical attention as soon as possible.

The following is a general guide to marine animals commonly encountered at Catalina.

Invertebrates

Nudibranchs & Related Gastropods

Common Name: Spanish shawl
Scientific Name: Flabellinopsis iodinea
Length: To 2" (5 cm)
Range: Vancouver Island, British Columbia to Cape San Quintin, Baja California

Common Name: Thick-horned aeolid
Scientific Name: Hermissenda crassicornis
Length: To 2" (5 cm)
Range: Vancouver Island, British Columbia to Cape San Quintin, Baja California

Common Name: Sea hare
Scientific Name: Aplysia californica
Length: To 18" (46 cm)
Range: Trinidad Bay, California to northern Baja California

Tube Worms

Common Name: Spiral-gilled tube worm
Scientific Name: Spirobranchus spinosus
Length: To 4" (10 cm)
Range: Alaska to California
Comments: Varieties of colors

Marine Snails and Other Shelled Animals

Common Name: Chestnut cowrie
Scientific Name: *Cypraea spadicea*
Length: To 2.6" (6.5 cm)
Range: Southern California to Baja California

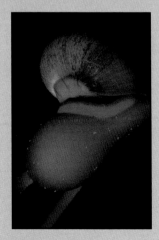

Common Name: Giant keyhole limpet
Scientific Name: *Megathura crenulata*
Length: To 6" (15 cm)
Range: Central California to Baja California

Common Name: Norris's Top Snail
Scientific Name: Norrisia norrisi
Length: To 55 mm in diameter
Range: Point Conception to Isla Asuncion, Baja, California

Common Name:	Giant rock scallop
Scientific Name:	Hinnites giganteus
Length:	To 10" (25.5 cm)
Range:	British Columbia to Baja California

Arthropods

Common Name:	California spiny lobster
Scientific Name:	*Panulirus interruptus*
Length:	To 2' (.6 m)
Range:	San Louis Obispo County, California to Rosalia Bay, Baja California

Anemones & Related Allies

Common Name:	Club-tipped anemone (Strawberry anemone)
Scientific Name:	*Corynactis californica*
Length:	Diameter to 1" (2.5 cm)
Range:	Point Arena, northern California to San Martin Island, Baja California

Common Name:	Yellow Colonial anemone
Scientific Name:	*Unidentified at time of printing*
Length:	Diameter up to .75" (2 cm)
Range:	British Columbia to central California

Common Name:	Tube anemone
Scientific Name:	*Pachycerianthis fimbriatus*
Length:	Length to 13" (35 cm)
Range:	British Columbia to San Diego, California
Comments:	Tentacle colors range from off-white to orange to black

Anemones & Related Allies (continued)

Common Name: Calif. Golden Gorgonian
Scientific Name: *Muricea californica*
Length: To 36" (91 cm)
Range: Point Conception to Baja California
Comments: Various species inhabit southern California waters

Common Name: Red Gorgonian
Scientific Name: *Lophogorgia chilensis*
Length: To 36" (91 cm)
Range: Monterey Bay to the San Benitos Islands, Baja California

Sea Stars & Related Echinoderms

Common Name: Pacific henricia
Scientific Name: *Henricia leviuscula*
Length: Radius to 3.6" (9 cm)
Range: Alaska to Baja California

Common Name: Comet star
Scientific Name: *Linckia columbiae*
Length: Radius to 3.6" (9 cm)
Range: Southern California to British Columbia

Common Name: Giant-Spined star
Scientific Name: *Pisaster giganteus*
Length: Radius to 22" (56 cm)
Range: Vancouver Island to Cedros Island, Baja California

Common Name: Sea urchin
Scientific Name: *Strongylocentrotus purpuratus*
Length: Diameter to 4" (10 cm)
Range: British Columbia to Baja California

Common Name: Sea cucumber
Scientific Name: *Parastichopus parvimensis*
Length: To 18" (46 cm)
Range: Carmel Bay, California to Cedros Island, Baja California

Marine Plants

Common Name: Giant kelp
Scientific Name: *Macrocystis pyrifera*
Length: Known to grow from depths of 130' (40 m) to the surface
Range: Alaska to Baja California
Comments: Can grow 2' (.6 m) per day if conditions are adequate

Vertebrates

Sharks & Rays

Common Name: Blue shark
Scientific Name: *Prionace glauca*
Length: To 12' (3.7 m)
Range: Gulf of Alaska to Chile

Common Name: Horn shark
Scientific Name: *Heterodontus francisci*
Length: Length to 3' (1 m)
Range: Central California to Gulf of California

Common Name: Pacific Angel shark
Scientific Name: *Squatina californica*
Length: Length to 5' (1.5 m)
Range: S. Alaska to Gulf of California
Comments: Once common at Catalina, the Angel Shark today is not frequently encountered.

Common Name: Bat ray
Scientific Name: *Myliobatis californica*
Length: Length to 6' (2 m)
Range: Oregon to Gulf of California
Comments: Common animal but not regularly encountered

Eels

Common Name: California moray eel
Scientific Name: *Gymonthorax mordax*
Length: To 5' (1.5 m)
Range: Point Conception, California to Bahia Magdalena Bay, B.C.

Photo Courtesy of Eric Hanauer

Scorpionfishes & Rockfishes

Common Name: California scorpionfish
Scientific Name: *Scorpaena guttata*
Length: To 17" (43 cm)
Range: Central California to Gulf of California
Comments: Venomous spines on dorsal fin

Common Name: Treefish
Scientific Name: *Sebastes serriceps*
Length: To 16" (40.5 cm)
Range: San Francisco to central Baja California

Basses

Common Name: Kelp bass
Scientific Name: *Paralabrax clathratus*
Length: To 28" (72 cm)
Range: Washington to southern Baja California

Wrasses

Common Name: California sheephead
Scientific Name: *Semicossyphus pulcher*
Length: To 3' (1 m)
Range: Monterey Bay, California to Cabo San Lucus, Baja California
Comments: Females characterized by pink colored body. Most females metamorphose into males at 7 to 8 years. Males characterized by black bodies with pink or red band in mid section.

Common Name: Rock wrasse
Scientific Name: *Halichoeres semicinctus*
Length: To 15" (38 cm)
Range: Pt. Conception, California to Guadalupe Island, Baja, B.C.
Comments: Male has dark bar rear of pectoral fin

Common Name: Señorita
Scientific Name: *Oxyjulis californica*
Length: To 12" (30.5 cm)
Range: N. California to Baja California

Damselfishes

Common Name: Blacksmith
Scientific Name: *Chromis punctipinnis*
Length: To 12" inches (30.5 cm)
Range: Monterey, California to Pt. San Pablo, Baja California

Common Name: Garibaldi
Scientific Name: *Hypsypops rubicundus*
Length: To 14" (35.5 cm)
Range: Monterey Bay, California to Bahia Magdalena Bay, Baja California
Comments: Protected species. Juveniles have iridescent blue spotting on their body. The blue disappears as the fish matures.

Kelpfishes

Common Name: Giant kelpfish
Scientific Name: *Heterostichus rostratus*
Length: To 2' (62 cm)
Range: British Columbia to Cabo San Lucus, Baja California
Comments: Some are pale green in color

Common Name: Island kelpfish
Scientific Name: *Alloclinus holderi*
Length: To 4" (10 cm)
Range: Santa Cruz Island, California to Central Baja California.

Gobies

Common Name: Bluebanded goby
Scientific Name: *Lythrypnus dalli*
Length: To 2.5" (1 cm)
Range: Morrow Bay, California to Guadalupe Island, Baja California

Common Name: Blackeye goby
Scientific Name: *Coryphopterus nicholsii*
Length: To 6' (.15 m)
Range: Northern British Colombia to C. Baja
Comments: Pale body • Big black eyes

Pinnipeds

Common Name: California sea lion
Scientific Name: *Zalophus californianus*
Length: Males to 8' (2.4 m) • Females to 6' (1.8 m)
Range:

Vancouver, British Columbia into Gulf of California

NOTES